A CENTURY WILD

1885
1985

Essays Commemorating
the
Centennial
of the
Adirondack Forest Preserve

Edited by Neal S. Burdick

A CENTURY WILD:
Essays Commemorating the Centennial of the Adirondack Forest Preserve

Library of Congress Catalog Card Number: 85-70991

ISBN 0-918517-06-0

The CHAUNCY PRESS

TURTLE POND ROAD
SARANAC LAKE. NEW YORK 12983

A Division of M & M Publications and Sails, Ltd.

DEDICATED

To All
Who Find Room In Their Lives
For Wild Places

Each of the essays in this anthology was commissioned as an article by *Adirondack Life* magazine. In most cases, the authors and/or the editor of this anthology have adapted the essays for use in this anthology, and in most cases the titles of the essays as they are presented here are not the same as those used when the essays appeared as articles in *Adirondack Life*.

Permission to reprint or adapt the articles has been granted by *Adirondack Life*.

CONTENTS

ACKNOWLEDGEMENTS

As is usually the case, many people had a hand in the evolution of this book. Credit for originating it goes to Norman Poltenson, who, as publisher of *Adirondack Life* magazine, conceived the idea of presenting in *Adirondack Life* a series of articles exploring the factors that led to the creation of the Adirondack Forest Preserve, to culminate with the publication of all of the articles in book form on the occasion of the centennial of the preserve in May of 1985.

The sequence of the series was mapped out at a meeting on a warm July day in 1983 in the conference room of the Department of Environmental Conservation Region G headquarters in Herkimer. Present at that meeting were two of the eventual contributors to the series, Norm Van Valkenburgh and Warder Cadbury, whose counsel was valuable in setting us on the right course.

Through the months when the articles appeared, issue by issue, in *Adirondack Life*, two editors — first Laurie Storey and later Bill Verner, who had been another author in the series — guided the project. It was Bill who suggested the title for the anthology, offering an alternative to an idea of mine that was so clumsy I've forgotten what it was. Bill was also instrumental in securing the illustrations.

I express deepest gratitude to the present management of *Adirondack Life* for granting me permission to continue the project on my own, and especially to Russ MacAusland and Jeff Kelly, the current publisher and editor, respectively, for their cooperation, assistance and encouragement. Another kind of encouragement came from the several authors and from our publishers, Murray and Madge Heller of The Chauncy Press, all of whose support was critical during those times when I wondered if all this effort would be worth it. Thanks also to Rita McCollum, who typed part of the manuscript. And of course I cannot forget my family — my wife, Barbara, and our children, Daniel and Melissa — who, understanding my lifelong interest in Adirondack history, never questioned the hours I spent in my study when they had every justification for doing so.

— Neal S. Burdick

PREFACE

This book is not a history of the Adirondacks. There are plenty of those. Nor is it a history of the Adirondack Forest Preserve. You can find that elsewhere, also. It is not even a history, in the normal sense of the word, of the creation of the Forest Preserve a century ago.

It is a collection of essays, orginally commissioned as articles in *Adirondack Life* magazine, by a number of experts in various areas of Adirondack history, in which they express their thoughts as to how certain elements of Adirondack history coalesced to create an atmosphere in which the Forest Preserve could come into being. The question they are investigating is more "why" than "how." That is the tougher question, and it lacks an easy answer, so you will not necessarily find consensus here. You will find a little repetition from one essay to the next; were this a more traditional history I would have edited it out, but for the most part I have not done so for fear of weakening each author's argument. Nor have I forced upon the whole, through the editing process, any prejudices of my own regarding what factors were more important than others. I believe it is safe to say that there is one thing upon which the authors agree: the Forest Preserve is a unique and priceless piece of New York's, and indeed America's, heritage.

What is this Forest Preserve of which we write, and why do we say it is unique? In simplest terms, the Forest Preserve is all those lands, mostly within the Adirondack and Catskill State Parks, that are owned and maintained as wild lands by the State of New York. (Devotees of the Catskills should not take offense because these essays are limited to the Adirondacks; remember that they were commissioned by a magazine whose subject is the Adirondacks.)

The Adirondack Forest Preserve and the Adirondack State Park are not synonymous, as many people mistakenly, but understandably, believe. Find the Adirondack Park on a state road map; it looks like a lopsided circle covering most of the northern third of the state. The Forest Preserve accounts for about 2.5 million acres, or 40 percent, of that circle. The rest is owned by an assortment of corporations, fish and game clubs, and individuals. Road maps do not indicate which land is state-owned and which is private, and for good reason: the Forest Preserve is not one large chunk of the park, but rather many small pieces scattered about as though they had been dropped from outer space. Any attempt to depict each parcel on a standard road map would render the map indecipherable. A specialized map from the Department of Environmental Conservation or the Adirondack Park Agency will show you the patchwork nature of the Forest Preserve.

But its disconnected character is not what is most significant about the Forest Preserve. What is significant about it is that part of it is mine (I share it with the twenty million other residents of New York State). Because the state owns it, it is public land, and I have as much right as the next person to use and enjoy it, as long as I abide by the strict guidelines that have been established to protect and perpetuate it. More than this, however, as a voting resident of the state I have as much say in what happens to the Forest Preserve as any other voter, including the governor. That is because in 1894, nine years after the legislature created the Forest Preserve, the legislature in effect offered the voters the opportunity to be the managers of the Forest Preserve by asking them if they wanted the Forest Preserve law to become part of the state's constitution. They did.

No bureaucrat or politician can change or wipe out the Forest Preserve with the stroke of a pen. The only way the Forest Preserve can be altered is through a constitutional amendment, which must be approved by two successive state legislatures and then by the voters. That may seem awfully complicated, but it is also rigorously egalitarian, and it ought to quell arguments that wilderness preservation, at least in New York State, is elitist. The uniqueness of the Adirondack Forest Preserve (and the Catskill Forest Preserve as well) is that its fate is entrusted to the people of the state in which it is located. It is their treasure to do with as they see fit.

The Forest Preserve was established one hundred years ago this month. But it was not a product of spontaneous generation. Like an embryo, it grew and was shaped for some time before it saw the light of day. It is the purpose of this book to explore, at least in small measure, that process of growing and shaping.

Neal S. Burdick
Canton, New York
May, 1985

Introduction

NEAL S. BURDICK

In the northwest quadrant of the Adirondacks, off a dirt road that parallels the St. Regis River between Paul Smiths and Santa Clara, stands Azure Mountain. Although its summit is only 2,518 feet above sea level, it offers a sweeping view that is unmatched by that from many higher peaks. To the north and northwest, the St. Lawrence River is a silver line cordoned by numerous towns, rich farmland and the telltale smoke of heavy industry. To the south and southeast can be seen many of the High Peaks of the Adirondacks: Whiteface, Marcy, Giant, Algonquin, the Sewards. More toward the east it is possible to see all the way to the last ridges before the land drops quickly to the Champlain Valley. Nearer at hand is a mosaic of forest, bog and pond that is interrupted but rarely by logging roads that emerge momentarily from the woods, only to be swallowed up again.

On top of Azure Mountain, precariously near the brink of its precipitous southwest face, sits an immense boulder. I suppose it is a glacial erratic, transported from who knows where by incomprehensible tons of ice and left behind like refuse when the ice retreated north 10,000 years ago. It has always fascinated me, mysterious monolith perched there like a gargoyle high on a Gothic spire.

Within sight of my rock, nearly upon the true summit of the mountain, stands a fire observer's tower. It has been abandoned for some years now, but I can remember, when I climbed this mountain as a child, winding my way up the spindly stairs — my heart nearer my throat with every step — and being shown by the observer how to pinpoint on his map a suspicious plume of smoke. It stands now like an erector set deserted by a young boy grown up. But it, too, fascinates me. Who built it — and how? What manner of men passed hours at a time in its crow's-nest of a cabin, scanning hundreds of miles of forest for signs of a fire that might destroy everything in sight? What fires never raged thanks to the use of this decaying hulk?

A tower and a rock. Man and nature. Most of Adirondack history over the past two centuries or more can be condensed in these two ideas. To trace Adirondack history is to trace man's relationship with nature.

Often when I am on the top of Azure Mountain (or any other Adirondack peak, for that matter) I imagine myself in a time machine. I travel back through Adirondack history . . .

It is 1903, and vast areas of the Adirondacks are burning. The fire tower isn't here, but the rock is. It is 1892, and most of the land I can see has just been designated the Adirondack State Park. The rock is here; it looks the same, whether it is suddenly part of a park or not. It is 1885, and the land has been stripped of its trees, by lumbermen who have left behind acre upon acre of stumps and mud. But in Albany, somewhere over the ridges fading to the south, the legislature has created the Adirondack Forest Preserve, and said the lumbering must stop, the lands in the Preserve remain forever wild. They don't look very wild now; man has conquered nature and claimed the spoils. But the rock is here.

It is 1792, and Alexander Macomb has purchased from the state most of the land I can see, for the purpose of speculation. It is 1535, and out of sight to the northeast Jacques Cartier, standing on high ground that will later be surrounded by the city of Montreal, is the first white man to see the Adirondacks. It is 1300, and a single aborigine appears momentarily in a clearing below me, perhaps stalking a deer, and the rock is here. It is 5,000 B.C., and the rock is here . . .

The difference between the rock and the tower, of course, is that the rock has been on top of Azure Mountain a lot longer than the tower has, and it will be there long after the last remnants of the tower have vanished. Over the centuries, man, with his purchases and his lumbering and his fires and his roads, has come and gone, but the rock has stayed. It measures time in milennia. I will not say it is permanent — a future Ice Age could move it just as surely as a previous one did — but I must concede that it is a lot more permanent than any of man's devices. The tower is a moment in the march of time, but the rock remains. And that is one of the lessons wilderness teaches.

I said Azure Mountain is part of the Forest Preserve, but not much of the Adirondack Park that I can see from its summit shares that distinction. Most of the northern and western parts of the Adirondacks are owned by individuals or companies, although from my perch on the mountaintop it all looks the same to me. That is because, for one reason or another, most of the private owners choose to keep their land in a relatively forested condition. Oh, logging does go on, but from a third of a mile up it is hardly visible.

But even though it may look the same, it is not likely that I would have the freedom to climb Azure Mountain whenever I feel like it were it not part of the Forest Preserve. I doubt whether a private owner would want just anybody walking up and down "his" mountain, picking his blueberries when they pepper the summit every August, enjoying his view, and so on. When the solons of a century ago created the Forest Preserve, they may have intended to do no more than satisfy the shipping interests of this state that the Erie Canal would always have water in it, but they also gave the rest of us a certain measure of freedom. The Erie Canal no longer plays the lead role in New York's economy, but we still have the freedom to hike the trails of the Forest Preserve.

I have known this Forest Preserve in many moods, many moments. I have stood on the tops of the tallest mountains in New York State and known what it is like, to paraphase the guide John Cheney, "to have all creation placed beneath my feet." I have stepped above timberline on more than one of the highest peaks and been devoured by a vicious wind. I have seen lightning blow an eighty-year-old tree into slivers in a second. I have looked in awe at trees that were seedlings before the Forest Preserve was conceived, before the lumbermen arrived, perhaps even before the first great purchases were made. I have heard waterfalls roar with the accumulated power of five months of winter storms. I have listened to the haunting song of the loon, and I have watched a pair of golden eagles soar on summer thermals. I have seen a deer drink calmly from a beaver pond, a coyote dart across a lonely road, and a snake swallow a frog.

To each of these I was an observer, one who happened to intercept eternity. Over eons yet to be, the mountains will continue to rise and fall and the wind to blow. The shattered tree will nourish its successors, and they will nourish theirs.

Water will continue to flow down to the valleys, shouting in spring and whispering in early fall. The deer will return to the pond, the coyote to hunt, and the snake to swallow frogs. I feel privileged to have witnessed these moments, but I feel more privileged knowing they will continue to occur long after I have passed by. There is that dimension of timelessness to the wilderness; it is greater by far than I.

One of my favorite sections of the Forest Preserve is the Five Ponds Wilderness Area south of Cranberry Lake. From its high spots, I can look in every direction and see nothing but forest, undulating like the sea, and imagine I am Daniel Boone beholding an unknown continent for the first time. Here, if I work at it, I can find true wilderness — not places that have been allowed to return to a wilderness condition, but places that have never been anything but wilderness. They have been spared settlement, fire, even the long tentacles of the logging railroads. Not even a purist can deny that these places are wilderness. There are few such places left, at least within easy reach of millions of people; without enlightened legislation it is likely there would be none.

At a lean-to by one of the Five Ponds, late one summer night a few years ago, seven college students and I watched with mingled amusement and distress while a very determined bear made off with some of our food. We, with all of our powers of reason, had cached the food from a tree limb high off the ground; he, with all of his powers of instinct, sensed we had not suspended it far enough out from the trunk of the tree. He was right, naturally, and so we lost a small amount of our food.

There was an undeniable simplicity in our situation that night. It came down to a matter of survival, for which we needed food (as did the bear, of course). Each of us, human and bear, wanted to obtain it as effortlessly as possible; each of us, bear and human, could have foraged for it had it not been available in a nylon bag at the end of a rope.

We later learned that at that very hour, halfway around the world, a jetliner was destroyed by a missile. That event helped us put our situation in perspective. Those doomed airplane passengers were not in control of their destinies, but we were. They, in one of the marvels of modern technology, could do nothing to save themselves, but we, in the virtually complete absence of civilization, had choices. There is that simplicity about the wilderness. I have heard it said that wilderness holds answers to questions we have not yet learned to ask; perhaps it also holds answers that we have not yet learned to see. And that is a good reason for preserving it.

But are abstract notions like permanence and simplicity reasons enough to preserve a wilderness? What matter if we have places that look the same as they did before our ancestors were born? Why should they be unchanged when we are ancestors? Is it not extravagant to set aside two and a half million acres of forest and say they should always be wild?

Less than one percent of the land in the forty-eight contiguous states of this nation is classified as wilderness, and much of that is of questionable quality because it is too close to a major highway, or has been lumbered too recently, or is subject to noise from an air route (parts of the Adirondack Forest Preserve suffer from these and other compromises, arguments about the distinction between "wilderness" and "wild land" notwithstanding). Given that a majority of the population regularly indicates that it wants wilderness, this does not seem extravagant. We could as easily ask if we have too many symphonies, or too many libraries, or too many books. The presence of wilderness is an indication not that civilization has failed to advance, but indeed that it has advanced so far that wilderness can once again be allowed to exist.

I would like to think we have progressed far enough that we no longer need fear the wilderness, no longer must have every ounce of its resources, no longer find it an impediment to our continued development. I would like to think we can afford to leave places for the deer to drink, the snake to swallow a frog, and a bear to outwit eight backpackers — and for their descendants to do the same things in the same places. I would like to think we can leave a huge, inscrutable rock near the edge of a cliff in the northern Adirondacks until some power other than our own decides to move it. I would like to think the wilderness will be allowed to outlive all of us.

x x x x x x

Prologue:
A Forest Preserve Chronology

NORMAN J. VAN VALKENBURGH

The history of the Adirondacks and the people who live in and visit the region is a familiar story. Similarly, the events leading to the discovery and settlement of these mountains and valleys are well known. The circumstances which brought about the various laws and constitutional provisions protecting the Adirondack Park and the lands and waters of the Adirondack Forest Preserve are also a part of the historical record, as is the language of those laws and of Article XIV — the famous "Forever Wild" clause — of New York's constitution.

As might be expected, the events leading to the law didn't happen all at once. What exists today evolved gradually over the years in what now can be recognized as a logical, step-by-step process. Milestones were reached and passed up to the 1885 creation of the Forest Preserve and thereafter as the government and people of the state refined and matured what has been called ". . . a unique example of conservation in the United States." In the briefest of terms, the preserve's chronology is here recounted.

The Formative Years

1535 — Jacques Carrier, French navigator and explorer, sails up the St. Lawrence River and from the heights at present-day Montreal looks southward to the Adirondacks.

1609 — Samuel de Champlain, French explorer, founder of Quebec and first French governor of Canada, sails up the Richelieu River and onto the waters now called Lake Champlain. On the western shore of the lake near Ticonderoga and in the shadow of the eastern slopes of the Adirondack Mountains, he fires his arquebus "loaded with four balls" and kills two of the Iroquois who were pursuing him and his party, thus precipitating the French and Indian War which will not end until 1760 on the Plains of Abraham.

In the fall of 1609, Henry Hudson, English navigator and explorer, sails the Half Moon up the river later to bear his name and reaches the head of tidewater near the future site of Albany. In years to come, the course of the Hudson River will be traced northerly through the Adirondacks to the upper slopes of the highest mountain in New York State.

1771 — Joseph Totten and Stephen Crossfield, New York City shipwrights, acting on behalf of the brothers Edward and Ebenezer Jessup, land speculators and then petitioners for a 40,000 acre tract of land at Luzerne (Warren County), petition, "In behalf of themselves and their associates," the Governor-in-Chief of the Province of New York for "lysence" to purchase a parcel of 800,000 acres from the Indian proprietors in what is now Essex, Hamilton, Herkimer and Warren counties. Later surveys determine Totten and Crossfield's Purchase to contain 1,150,000 acres.

1779 — In the midst of the American Revolution (1775-1783), New York State enacts the so-called Act of Attainder (Chapter 24, Laws of 1779) declaring that all lands belonging to the Crown of Great Britain on July 8, 1776 be "forever after . . . vested in the people of this state." This passes title (along with other lands across the state) to about 7,000,000 acres in and around the Adirondacks to the state.

1784 — The New York legislature passes Chapter 60 of the Laws of 1784, the first of a series of laws establishing easy procedures and cheap prices under which the state can effect the "speedy sale" of the "waste and unappropriated lands within the state." These lands are those principally in the Adirondack Mountains acquired by the state pursuant to the earlier Act of Attainder.

1792 — Alexander Macomb completes the purchase of 3,635,600 acres of "waste and unappropriated" lands from the state. This incorporates nearly all of the northerly and westerly Adirondack Mountains and spreads across Franklin, St. Lawrence, Herkimer, Hamilton, Lewis, Jefferson and Oswego counties.

1806 — The Salmon River (Franklin County) is declared, by law, to be a public highway so that logs can be driven down it without interference from the shoreline landowners. This is followed by similar laws declaring other Adirondack waterways to be public highways, thus facilitating the removal of timber from and encouraging widespread lumbering in the mountains.

1808 — The Legislature passes Chapter 191 of the Laws of 1808, making it a misdemeanor for anyone to cut down or destroy the "public woods in the county of Essex." This is the first legislative attempt to preserve the forests of the Adirondack Mountains.

1837 — Professor Ebenezer Emmons, geologist in charge of the natural history survey of the "northern wilderness," climbs the High Peak of Essex (the highest summit in New York State) and names it Mt. Marcy for Governor William Learned Marcy, proponent of the survey. Emmons, in his report to the legislature, "proposed to call . . . the cluster of mountains in the neighborhood . . . the Adirondack group, a name by which a well known tribe of Indians who once hunted here may be commemorated."

1838 — Professor William C. Redfield, geologist and meteorologist with the Emmons survey, publishes "Some Account of Two Visits to the Mountains in Essex County, New York, in the Years 1836 and 1837; with a Sketch of the Northern Sources of the Hudson" in *Family Magazine,* the first "popular" writing about the Adirondack Mountains and the forerunner to a vast literature about the mountains and its people.

1839 — Charles Cromwell Ingham, founder of the National Academy of Design, who had accompanied the Emmons survey to Mt. Marcy, first exhibits his oil painting " The Great Adirondack Pass," beginning a tradition of Adirondack landscape painting that will be followed by the Hudson River School of painters and other artists to the present.

1848 — The Sacketts Harbor and Saratoga Railroad Company is incorporated by Chapter 207, Laws of 1848, which also entitles the company to purchase up to 250,000 acres of state land in Hamilton and Herkimer counties, to mortgage such lands and to sell the timber on them for capital to construct and operate a railroad from Saratoga Springs to Sacketts Harbor in Jefferson County. This is the first of a series of similar laws seeking to bring a business entity into (and through) the Adirondacks at the expense of the public lands and the forests on them.

1857 — Samuel H. Hammond, an Albany journalist, publishes *Wild Northern Scenes; or Sporting Adventures with the Rifle and Rod* and states therein (speaking of the Adirondacks), "Had I my way, I would mark out a circle of a

Ebenezer Emmons
Credit: The Adirondack Museum, Blue Mountain Lake, N.Y.

hundred miles in diameter, and throw around it the protecting aegis of the Constitution. I would make it a forest forever." This is the first published advocacy for preservation and constitutional protection of the Adirondack Mountains.

1866 — The first land acquisitions by the state in the Adirondacks are authorized by Chapter 748 of the Laws of 1866, which appropriates $8,500 for the purchase of seven hundred acres of woodland in Clinton County "for the purpose of obtaining necessary supplies of wood for the state prison."

1870 — Verplanck Colvin, a self-taught land surveyor from Albany, reaches the summit of Mt. Seward in Franklin County and in his report of the expedition to the Board of Regents of the State of New York makes the plea ". . . that these forests should be preserved; and for posterity should be set aside, this Adirondack region, as a park for New York . . ."

1873 — The Commission of State Parks, appointed under the provisions of Chapter 848 of the Laws of 1872 "to inquire into the expediency of providing for vesting in the state the title to the timbered regions lying within the counties of Lewis, Essex, Clinton, Franklin, St. Lawrence, Herkimer and Hamilton and converting the same into a public park," makes its report to the legislature, stating, "we are of opinion that the protection of a great portion of that forest from wanton destruction is absolutely and immediately required."

1883 — Chapter 13 of the Laws of 1883 is enacted, prohibiting the further sale of lands belonging to the state in Clinton, Essex, Franklin, Fulton, Hamilton, Herkimer, Lewis, Saratoga, St. Lawrence and Warren counties.

1884 — A forestry commission is authorized under Chapter 551 of the Laws of 1884 ". . . to investigate and report a system of forest preservation." This commission (called the Sargent Commission for its chairman, Charles Sprague Sargent, professor of arboriculture at Harvard University) recommends, in its report to the comptroller of the state of New York in January of 1885, a law creating a forest preserve of the state lands in eleven Adirondack counties to "be forever kept as wild forest lands."

The Official Years

1885 — The Adirondack and Catskill Forest Preserves are created on May 15 by enactment of Chapter 283 of the Laws of 1885, requiring that "All the lands now owned or which may hereafter be acquired by the state of New York . . ." in eleven Adirondack and three Catskill counties ". . . be forever kept as wild forest lands. They shall not be sold, nor shall they be leased or taken by any person or corporation, public or private." Provisions in the same law establish a three-man Forest Commission to administer and be responsible for the 681,000-acre Adirondack Forest Preserve and the 34,000-acre Catskill Forest Preserve.

1887 — Chapter 475 of the Laws of 1887 is enacted to redefine the duties of the Forest Commission to empower it to sell ". . . separate small parcels or tracts wholly detached from the main portion of the Forest Preserve" and to sell the timber thereon. This is the first of a number of laws enacted at the urging of the commission to lessen the restrictions on the land of the Forest Preserve.

Oneida County is added to the list of counties constituting the Adirondack

Forest Preserve. An 1888 law omits Oneida County from the listing. However, this oversight is corrected by an 1889 law which again includes Oneida County. The same twelve-county listing continues today.

1890 — $25,000 is provided to "... purchase lands so located within such counties as include the forest preserve ..." This is the first specific appropriation for the acquisition of land to add to and expand the Forest Preserve.

1892 — Chapter 707 of the Laws of 1892 establishes a 2,800,000-acre Adirondack Park. The boundaries of the Park are delineated on a map by a blue line, establishing a tradition whereby the Adirondack Park boundary is always shown on official state maps by a blue line.

1893 — Reacting to reports and investigations of irregularities within the three-man Forest Commission, the commission is replaced with a new five-man Forest Commission. The law taking such action, however, provides authority for the sale of timber from the Forest Preserve, the sale of some of the lands of the Forest Preserve, and the lease of five-acre lots on the Preserve for camps and cottages. All this sets the stage for the proponents of a more restrictive Forest Preserve as they prepare for the Constitutional Convention to convene the following spring.

1894 — The Constitutional Convention approves a new Article VII, which states, "The lands of the state, now owned or hereafter acquired, constituting the Forest Preserve as now fixed by law, shall be forever kept as wild forest lands. They shall not be leased, sold or exchanged, or be taken by any corporation, public or private, nor shall the timber thereon be sold, removed or destroyed." This proposal (combined with other amendments from the Convention) is approved by the people and becomes effective on January 1, 1895.

1895 — The Fisheries Commission, the Game Commission and the Forest Commission are combined into a single Fisheries, Game and Forest Commission which is assigned the responsibility (among others) for administration of the Forest Preserve.

1900 — The Fisheries, Game and Forest Commission is reconstituted as the Forest, Fish and Game Commission.

1903 — An intensive drought, high winds and other conditions produce widespread forest fires across the Adirondacks. These and equally destructive forest fires in the next few years bring about an expansion of the state forest fire control force, more stringent laws to prevent such fires and, in 1910, the first fire observation towers on the higher Adirondack (and Catskill) mountain peaks.

1911 — The Forest, Fish and Game Commission is reconstituted as the Conservation Commission. Established within it is the Division of Lands and Forests as the agency responsible for administration of the Forest Preserve.

1912 — The Adirondack Park is expanded to 4,054,000 acres with the Blue Line following the outside limits of the "Great Forest of Northern New York" and including all private lands as well as the state lands in the Park.

1913 — The Constitution is amended to provide that up to 3 percent of the total acreage of the Forest Preserve can be used as water reservoirs for the purpose of municipal water supply, state canals and regulation of the flow of streams.

1916 — A $7.5 million bond issue for the acquisition of lands for addition to the Adirondack and Catskill Forest Preserves is approved and adds 245,000 acres to the Adirondack Forest Preserve over the next ten years.

1918 — The Constitution is amended to allow the use of Forest Preserve land in the construction of a state highway from Saranac Lake to Tupper Lake (now Route 3) to Blue Mountain Lake (now Route 30) to Old Forge (now Route 28).

1920 — The first public campgrounds are established in the Adirondacks.

1924 — A $15 million bond issue to expand state parks is approved, of which $5 million is allocated to acquire lands to expand the Forest Preserve in the Adirondack and Catskill Parks. These funds provide for the addition of 273,000 acres to the Adirondack Forest Preserve over the next twenty years.

1927 — The Constitution is amended to allow the construction of a state highway (now Route 431) across Forest Preserve lands from Wilmington to the top of Whiteface Mountain.

The Conservation Commission is renamed the Conservation Department.

1931 — The Adirondack Park is enlarged to encompass a total of 5,600,000 acres within the Blue Line.

The Constitution is amended to permit the acquisition of lands for and the establishment of reforestation areas and forest tree nurseries across the state outside the Adirondack and Catskill Parks, and the "cutting, selling or removing of the trees, timber, forest products and other materials" from these lands. Additional provisions of this amendment provide for annual appropriations of funds to acquire lands for the purposes permitted.

1932 — A proposed amendment to the Constitution to authorize the construction of paths, trails, campsites and camping facilities (so-called "closed cabins") on the Forest Preserve is defeated.

The III Winter Olympiad is celebrated at Lake Pacid following a major controversy and a series of lawsuits over the siting of "a bobsleigh run or slide" on Forest Preserve land. The bobrun is finally constructed on an easement acquired by the state on the slopes of Mt. Van Hoevenberg.

1933 — The Constitution is amended to permit the construction of a state highway (now Route 30) from Indian Lake to Speculator.

The Civilian Conservation Corps is organized by the federal government. A number of camps of the corps are established across the state with some on Forest Preserve land in the Adirondacks. Much good work is done by the corps, including construction and improvement of public campsites and trails, before it is disbanded in 1942.

1935 — The fifty-year anniversary of the establishment of the Forest Preserve is celebrated.

1938 — As the result of the 1938 Constitutional Convention, Article VII of the Constitution is recodified to Article XIV and partly reworded with no change, however, in the "forever wild" language. The new Article XIV is grouped with the major part of the Constitution proposed by the Convention and is adopted at the November 8 general election.

1941 — The Constitution is amended to allow the construction of "20 miles of ski trails 30 to 80 feet wide" on Whiteface Mountain.

1947 — The Constitution is amended to permit the construction of "20 miles of ski trails 30 to 80 feet wide" on Belleayre Mountain in the Catskills and, 30 miles of ski trails" of the same width on Gore, South and Pete Gay Mountains.

1950 — A severe wind storm sweeps across the state and creates a blowdown of timber on 424,000 acres of Adirondack land including parts of the Forest Preserve.

1953 — Reacting to a proposal by the Black River Regulating District, supported by the U.S. Corps of Engineers, to construct a dam and reservoir on the Moose River at Panther Mountain in Herkimer County, the voters of the state amend the Constitution so as to remove regulation of the flow of streams as a permissible use of 3 percent of the total Forest Preserve, as had been authorized in 1913.

1955 — A proposed amendment to the Constitution to permit the use of 1,500 acres of Forest Preserve for the Panther Mountain reservoir is defeated.

1956 — The Adirondack Park is enlarged to a total of 5,693,500 acres.

1957 — The Constitution is amended to permit the sale, exchange or dedication to another use of those so-called "detached parcels" of Forest Preserve lands of less than ten acres in size inside the Adirondack and Catskill counties but outside the Adirondack and Catskill Parks.

A second amendment is approved to permit the use of up to four hundred acres of Forest Preserve to relocate, reconstruct or maintain a total of not more than fifty miles of existing state highways.

1959 — The Constitution is amended to allow the use of up to three hundred acres of Forest Preserve to construct the Northway (now Interstate Route 87).

1960 — A $75 million Park and Recreation Land Acquisition Bond Act is approved. Funding from this bond issue and a supplemental one of $25 million approved in 1962 provides $2.6 million to acquire 102,000 acres of land as additions to the Adirondack Forest Preserve.

The Joint Legislative Committee on Natural Resources, which had been asked in 1952 to look into problems affecting the Forest Preserve and to recommend needed solutions, begins its study of the possibility of designating certain parts of the Preserve as wilderness areas.

1961 — The Joint Legislative Committee on Natural Resources completes its wilderness area studies and recommends that twelve such areas be established within the Adirondack Forest Preserve.

1963 — The Constitution is amended to allow the exchange of ten acres of Forest Preserve land for thirty acres of "true forest land" owned by the village of Saranac Lake to "provide for refuse disposal."

1965 — The Constitution is amended to allow the exchange of twenty-eight acres of Forest Preserve land for thirty acres of land owned by the Town of Arietta "for the extension of the runway and landing strip of the Piseco airport."

1967 — A proposal to amend the Constitution to allow for the construction of thirty miles of ski trails on Hoffman, Blue Ridge and Peaked Hill mountains (in

Essex County) is defeated.

A plan is proposed by Laurance S. Rockefeller, brother of then Governor Nelson A. Rockefeller, to create a 1.7 million-acre Adirondack Mountains National Park from 1.1 million acres of Forest Preserve and 600,000 acres of private land in the center of the Adirondack Park.

1968 — Governor Nelson A. Rockefeller appoints a Temporary Study Commission on the Future of the Adirondacks to develop recommendations to guide future use of the public and private lands within the Adirondack Park.

1969 — The Constitution is amended to create the State Nature and Historical Preserve outside the Adirondack and Catskill Forest Preserve counties to consist of properties to be acquired and protected "because of their natural beauty, wilderness character, or geological, ecological or historical significance."

1970 — The Department of Environmental Conservation (DEC) is created as a merger of the Conservation Department and parts of other state agencies.

1971 — The Adirondack Park Agency (APA) is created with responsibility for preparing plans for use of the public and private lands within the Park and for administering parts of such plans when finalized.

1972 — The Adirondack Park State Land Master Plan is completed by the APA in consultation with the DEC, and is adopted. It divides the state lands within the Park into a number of specific areas and classifications, including fifteen wilderness areas totaling nearly one million acres.

The Environmental Quality Bond Act is approved to provide (among other fundings) $44 million for the acquisition of lands to consolidate and provide additional access to the Adirondack Forest Preserve. Land acquisitions under this bond act are continuing, with 67,000 acres so far acquired for addition to the Adirondack Forest Preserve, at a cost of $14 million.

The Adirondack Park is expanded to a total of 5,927,600 acres.

1973 — The Constitution is amended to raise the size limitation of the so-called detached parcels of Forest Preserve outside the Adirondack and Catskill Parks which can be sold, exchanged or dedicated to another use from ten to one hundred acres.

The Adirondack Party Agency completes the Adirondack Park Land Use and Development Plan. With its adoption by law, the private lands within the Park are zoned into various categories with each being restricted as to type and density of use.

1979 — The Constitution is amended to allow the exchange of up to 8,500 acres of Adirondack Forest Preserve for land of equal value owned by the International Paper Company at Perkins Clearing in Hamilton County.

1980 — The XIII Winter Olympiad is celebrated at Lake Placid.

1980 +— Acid precipitation looms as the greatest threat the natural resources and aesthetics of the Adirondack Mountains have ever faced.

1983 — The Constitution is amended to allow the exchange of ten acres of Forest Preserve land and the "historic grouping of buildings" thereon with Sagamore Institute, Inc. for "approximately two hundred acres of wild forest land located within the Adirondack Park."

1985 — The centennial of the Adirondack (and Catskill) Forest Preserve is celebrated.

Forerunners

WILLIAM K. VERNER

On May 15, 1885, Governor David B. Hill signed into law an act "to establish a forest commission, and to define its powers and duties, and for the preservation of the forests." In addition to providing for an appointed three-member forest commission and spelling out in considerable detail its duties as to the maintenance, protection, and promotion of future forest growth in New York State, the law established a forest preserve to consist of most lands "now owned or which may hereafter be acquired by the State" in eleven Adirondack and three Catskill counties. It directed that "the lands now or hereafter constituting the forest preserve shall be forever kept as wild forest lands. They shall not be sold, nor shall they be leased or taken by any person or corporation, public or private."

Although it is not our purpose here to dwell upon what has taken place since 1885, it is well to consider the almost talismanic ring of the phrase "forever wild" and how, from the moment of its introduction into the legal parlance of New York State, it harbored seeds of self-fulfilling prophecy. Intended in its own time primarily to provide a tentative means of achieving such utilitarian goals as watershed protection and a future timber supply, the phrase today has come to signify an end in itself, or, if not strictly that, to indicate a means for achieving social goals rather far removed from the practicalities of water and timber.

Westward

Jacques Cartier was the first European of record to lay eyes upon what, some three hundred years later, would be called the Adirondack Mountains. Though specifically in the service of Francis I of France and searching for a passage to the Orient, Cartier was equally and more importantly a part of that fifteenth century phenomenon in which the encounter of Europeans from the West and aborigines whose ancestors had come from the East completed human encirclement of the Earth. Cartier worked his way up the St. Lawrence River to an Indian settlement called Hochelaga in the fall of 1535. The Indians guided Cartier and his party to the top of a mountain, which, in the 1580 translation of John Florio, "we named *Mount Roiall* . . . ." When we were on the toppe of it, we might discerne, and plainely see thirtie leagues off. On the North side of it there are manye hilles to be seene, running Weaste and Easte, and as manye more on the Southe, amongst and betweene the which the Countrey is as fayre and as pleasaunte as possiblye can be seene, being leavell, smoothe, and verye playne, fitte to be husbanded and tilled . . ."

The French would not establish themselves upon the St. Lawrence until early in the following century, with the arrival of Samuel de Champlain. His encounter with Iroquois Indians near Ticonderoga in 1609 would help define the opposition of French and Algonquin interests to the north, against those of the British and Iroquois to the south over the next 150 years. As a natural buffer between these spheres of influence, the Adirondacks gained a far longer life as a *de facto* wilderness than might otherwise have been the case.

Despite French settlements on Lake Champlain later that century and into the next, despite the French and Indian Wars, important conflicts of which were played out in the Adirondacks in the mid-eighteenth century, and despite more of the same during the Revolutionary War, the Adirondacks remained beyond the reach of knowledge by either French or British interests. There is perhaps no better formulation of the situation than that provided in 1776 by Thomas Pownall in his *Topographical Description of North America,* a revision of material prepared in 1755 by Lewis Evans to accompany his important *General Map of the Middle British Colonies.* In attempting to describe the sources of the Hudson River, Pownall was forced to conclude, "rather to mark my Ignorance than presuming to give Information," that "the Country, lying to the West of these Lakes [George and Champlain], bounded on the North West by Canada River [the St. Lawrence], and on the South by the Mohawks River, called by the Indians Couxsachrage, which signifies the Dismal Wilderness or Habitation Of Winter, is a triangular, high mountainous Tract, very little known to the Europeans; and although a hunting Ground of the Indians, yet either not much known to them, or, if known, very wisely by them kept from the Knowledge of the Europeans. It is said to be a broken unpracticable Tract," Pownall concluded. "I own I could never learn any Thing about it . . . ."

It would be more than fifty years after the Revolution before people would know much more about the region, especially its central core. Anxious to gain liquidity for its empty coffers, the State of New York launched upon a veritable selling spree of lands which had come into its ownership as a result of the successful outcome of the Revolutionary War. Of the approximately seven million acres of lands acquired under the Act of Attainder of 1779, the state disposed of some 1,150,000 acres in redistributing the Totten and Crossfield Purchase, 665,000 acres as bounty lands offered to veterans, and, in 1791, 3,625,200 acres to Alexander McComb and associates. These grants, in turn, the new owners did their best to dispose of to settlers, mainly from New England, and indeed, by 1820 practically all lands once owned by the state had been sold off. Some settlement began taking place, but most of this was limited to the lower and more agriculturally rich areas surrounding the high mountains and lakes of the interior. Only a handful of settlers penetrated the central Adirondacks.

Adirondack

Among the pioneers of the interior were the people associated with what was to become the Adirondack Iron & Steel Company. A look at the activities and personalities associated with this mining venture is instructive not only as to attitudes characteristic of the second quarter of the nineteenth century, but also for themes that would contribute to the creation of "forever wild" a half century later. Some viewpoints, not the least the hope of carving a mining fortune out of the virgin deposits of the central Adirondacks, are by no means surprising; others are. One thing is certain: it was a remarkably tight-knit group of individuals in the 1830s who were instrumental in putting the Adirondacks on the map both literally and figuratively.

A key figure in this story was Archibald McIntrye, a Scot by birth, resident of

New York City and Albany, active in state politics throughout the first half of the century, and New York State Controller from 1806 to 1821. In 1809, he and some associates developed the North Elba Iron and Steel company near the present village of Lake Placid just north of the High Peaks. Although the operation was not a financial success, it provided them a base of operations for further discoveries. In 1826, David Henderson, who was to become McIntyre's son-in-law, following the tip of an Abenaki Indian trapper, led a party south from North Elba, through Indian Pass ("the Notch," as they sometimes referred to it), and stumbled upon extensive iron ore beds at the headwaters of the Hudson River near Newcomb. Over the next few years, and taking full advantage of their contacts in the legislative halls of Albany, McIntyre and his people acquired several thousand acres surrounding the ore beds and gained state approval and financing for the building of a road to connect the remote and budding enterprise with Lake Champlain to the east.

Looking forward himself to a visit to Essex County and an inspection of the new site in 1830, McIntyre wrote to a friend that he relied "much on the benign influence of the mountain air of Essex on my constitution. I long to be snuffing it." Again, in February, 1833, following another trip to the woods the previous fall, McIntrye commented on this positive influence: "I have reason to be very thankful for the great improvement to my health, which I attribute to my Northern Jaunt .... I wish we had suitable roads to, and suitable accomodations [sic] at 'McIntyre,' for our families to go there. I have no doubt it would be beneficial for them to spend a month or two there annually."

McIntyre had hit upon two themes that would become fundamental to Adirondack life in future years — the health-giving potential of the region and its suitability for family vacations. Still, McIntyre's principal concern was with the economic potential of the mine, and by June he had developed serious doubts about the venture. "I confess that I am at times alarmed & disheartened with this same concern of ours, and afraid that it may turn out another Elba," he wrote, referring to the North Elba mine failure of years before. "For the ore has not been tested, the roads are abominable, and coal wood in the vicinity is very scarce ...." A year later he was no more optimistic: "The more I think of our unfortunate concern, the more I am satisfied of the egregious folly of our whole proceedings, and the necessity of making what can be made from the wreck as speedily as possible."

In an attempt to spread the financial burden for his father-in-law, David Henderson brought some visitors to the mine in the summer of 1836. They included potential investors David C. Colden, for whom the lake and mountain north of the iron works were eventually named, and William C. Redfield, a prominent meteorologist. By that fall, McIntyre was able to hope that these gentlemen might be able to "take hold of our Iron Concern, and make the most of it for themselves and us."

As it turned out, neither Colden nor Redfield invested in the project, but their visit, and Redfield's return the following summer, contributed in important ways to making it possible for the venture to continue. Another source of help was the State Natural History Survey which Governor William L. Marcy had authorized in 1836 and which had begun field work that summer under a geologist named Ebenezer Emmons.

While exploring in the upper reaches of the Hudson, Henderson and Redfield discovered in the distance, still above them, mountains, one in particular far higher than they had anticipated. Meanwhile, from the summit of Whiteface Mountain a little later that summer of 1836, Emmons and an assistant, James Hall, noted the same mountains lying to their south and concluded that one or more of them were higher than the summit upon which they found themselves. Members of both parties subsequently agreed that they would continue their explorations the following summer, using the mining village as their base of operations.

Anticipation of the 1837 expedition ran high. In the spring, Henderson wrote McIntyre that it looked entirely possible that Governor Marcy himself might be joining them. Other thoughts occupied his mind as well. "The territory is getting into so much notice," he emphasized, "that I verily believe, were a railroad to be made from [Lake Champlain into the mine], and a large public house erected — it would become a fashionable resort for the summer months — the notch," referring to Indian Pass, "being the greatest curiosity in the country next to the Falls of Niagara. If Niagara be the prince of waterfalls — the other exhibits the prince of precipices." To health and the family vacation, McIntyre and Henderson could now add the resort business as another potential for the Adirondacks.

Although the Governor was unable to come north that summer, others did — among them artists Asher B. Durand and Thomas Cole, along with their wives, who vacationed and painted at Schroon Lake. Another artist, Irish-born portraitist Charles C. Ingham, joined Ebenezer Emmons, James Hall, David Henderson, William Redfield and others at the mining village in midsummer, and on Saturday, August 5, they reached the summit of a peak that they realized with certainty was the highest in the state. Emmons named it for the absent Governor Marcy who had been instrumental in creating the state Natural History Survey, which had brought many of them to that spot, and James Hall made some notes on the summit that day, which he got into the mail to the *Albany Daily Advertiser* a few days later.

In the summer heat of New York City, a one-legged writer and editor named Charles Fenno Hoffman was brooding about two short notices that appeared in the weekly *New York Mirror* with which he was associated. One of them had no bearing on northern New York whatsoever, or wouldn't have until events nearly 150 years later in the Adirondacks would suggest that it had pertinence after all. The piece had to do with a proposed suburban housing development on Staten Island that called for uniform housing lots. "Can anything be more preposterous or insulting to common sense," someone wrote, probably Hoffman himself, "than asking a man to build a *country seat* upon a piece of ground twenty-five by a hundred! . . . Why will not our village-making projectors take a leaf from John Bull's book, and get up something upon the plan of 'Regent's Park,'" the reference being to a London housing plan. The writer went on to suggest a landscape design of varying lot sizes (some smaller, some larger), "leaving all the rest in commons" and subject to certain regulations. Here were some of the principles of flexible land use planning that would come to the Adirondacks years later, and here too was the concept of "the commons," open space lands reserved out of development for all to enjoy.

The other item in the *Mirror* that Saturday in August reported on Hall's note to the Albany newspaper — that he and his companions had found themselves at the headwaters of the Hudson River "among a notable group of mountains, which ought to be henceforth called after the ancient aboriginal name of the river," namely the Mohegan Mountains, in Hall's opinion.

Over the next few days Hoffman must have found himself preoccupied by both of these short notices and with the northern American landscape art of Thomas Cole. The evidence is in a literary exercise that appeared in the *Mirror* on September 2 under Hoffman's byline. Called "The Last Man: A Chapter in the Style of the Day," Hoffman's piece again condemned the unimaginative Staten Island development plan, referred to the "Mohegan mountains, where, wholly unnoticed by the learned gentlemen who have been tracing the sources of the Hudson in that quarter, I have accompanied the surveying party over many a romantick tract" in imagination if not in fact, and not far from the place where "the magick pencil of Cole" had been busied.

Imagination proving insufficient, Hoffman was on his way north within a week, and throughout the latter half of September and all of October the *Mirror* ran his personal dispatches concerning "Scenes at the Sources of the Hudson." Hoffman reported riding in a buckboard and rowing by boat to reach the mining village, told of his guides John Cheney and Harvey Holt, reported talks of moose and deer hunts, and relished the loneliness and seclusion of the iron works area. "I plead guilty to a sort of miserly feeling as regards natural scenery," he wrote. "I love it most when hoarded, as it were, away from the eye of the profane" and still immune from having become "a hunt of Fashion." He also camped out on the spot where, according to Cheney, Ingham had painted Indian Pass earlier that summer, a site that "I doubt not . . . will become as favourite a place of resort as Lake George, Trenton Falls, or Niagara." Hoffman also experienced an earthquake at Indian Pass which suggested to him "the *unfinished state of the country*" (his emphasis), but, his physical disability preventing his personal ascent of Mount Marcy (for which, at this time, he suggested the alternate name of *Ta-ha-wus*), he had to depend upon Cheney's assertion that being on its summit "makes a man feel what it is to have all creation placed beneath his feet. . . ." He also made an observation that many following him were to repeat, namely that the Erie Canal, completed some twelve years before and thereby "carrying emigration westward," had retarded settlement in the mountains.

By November, Hoffman, who had found it "strange to find so wild a district in 'one of the old thirteeners,' the 'empire state of New-York,'" was back in the city in the company of David Colden and other members of the St. Nicholas Society offering a toast at Delmonico's to "Our State: The battlefield of America in three wars. The elastick spirit of her adventurous sons" has "converted the arena of arms into the commercial highways of nations."

As Hoffman had popularized northern New York in the fall of 1837, so did others continue the process in the spring of 1838. Redfield, who had sent a preliminary notice of the explorations to New York's *Journal of Commerce* (August 18, 1837), published a detailed account of his trips "to the mountains in Essex County" in both the *American Journal of Science* and *The Family Magazine,* and Emmons submitted an official report to the legislature that was accompanied by lithographic reproductions of sketches made by both Ingham and himself. It was in this report that Emmons recommended calling the mountains "the Adirondack group," thereby putting to rest earlier suggestions by Hall and others. Later that year, the *Mirror* reviewed a new painting by Thomas Cole on exhibit at the National Academy of Design, a product of his sojourn the year before with Durand — "Schroon Mountain," notable for "its remarkable fidelity to nature," its "gorgeous" fall foliage, as the work of "a true lover of his own native land" (overlooking the fact that Cole had been born in England) and as "a faithful and bold delineator of all her wild scenery," by an artist who "stands and will, we think, continue to stand, unrivalled and alone."

That fall of 1838, a packet ship was launched on New York City's East River. It was christened *Adirondack,* and shortly thereafter William Henry Seward was elected governor. In January, 1839, shortly after Governor Seward's inauguration, guide John Cheney paid a visit to Albany and delivered to Archibald McIntyre, owner of the Adirondack Iron Works, meat from a moose he had hunted down near the mining village a short time before. Delighted with the gift, McIntyre presented some to the new governor, who included it on the menu of a banquet which McIntyre attended. The rest he sent down to New York where Henderson, Hoffman, Colden, Ingham, and others gathered to celebrate a midwinter reunion. That spring, Ingham's large painting, "The Great Adirondack Pass: Painted on the Spot," was exhibited at the National Academy. Just over three hundred years after Cartier's orginal sighting, the Adirondacks finally were on the map and becoming well fixed in the public mind. Thanks, in part, to the recent publicity and to the scientific support of Emmons, Archibald McIntyre and his associates moved forward with further development of their iron works.

The Wilderness Years

Until the 1830s the Adirondacks had been, from time immemorial, a vast wilderness, some peripheral agricultural development and a few scattered interior settlements perhaps excepted, but the region had lacked cultural significance. Few, if any, people thought of the region as an entity, and certainly the public at large did not perceive it as such. Following the ascent and naming of Mount Marcy, the wilderness, at least that of the central Adirondacks, was to remain relatively undisturbed for some decades to come but with the difference that, now, the public had a sense of its geographical identity.

Further field trips by Ebenezer Emmons helped to refine this sense of definition, especially his final trip of 1840 when he, zoologist James DeKay, artist John W. Hill, and others made their way north from the newly popular fishing resort of Lake Pleasant to Indian Lake and then to Blue Mountain, Raquette, Long, and the Saranac lakes. When he published his comprehensive geological report, illustrated by Hill's lithographs in 1842, Emmons laid aside his geologist's hammer for a moment to comment on some of the non-scientific aspects of his findings, particularly with respect to the lakes area. "I would remember," he wrote, "that in a community constituted like ours, many individuals require recreation during certain seasons." He went on to suggest that his discoveries opened up "a new field for relaxation from business — one which has peculiar advantages and many resources for restoring health and spirits, such as are unknown at the more fashionable watering places. The breezes of Hamilton [County] are invigorating; the lake scenery is magnificent, and the exercise it calls forth is healthful; and the invalid who, after reaching these romantic wilds, makes a rational use of the forests and lakes and the skies which invest them, and returns dissatisfied with what he has received, I should pronounce not only difficult to please, but mistaken in the objects of his search and the character of his wants."

One of many who came to the Adirondacks in this period on the terms Emmons had suggested was John Todd, a Congregational minister from Pittsfield, Massachusetts. In 1841 he had visited what was later to become the University of Vermont at Burlington to give an address and, feeling somewhat worn out by his work, joined mathematics professor Farrand N. Benedict in a jaunt to the Adirondacks. Benedict owned land in the central region, and he had provided Emmons with important information about the mountains some years earlier. As for Todd, although he certainly relished the outdoor life, something in him — his proselytizing instinct — was not fully satisfied by this or by his subsequent trips to the central Adirondacks and to Long Lake. What Long Lake needed was a church and a better road to provide access so that "population will roll in" and "when the day shall arrive in which these forests shall be cut down . . . , there shall be a virtuous, industrious and Christian population" there. "I have no doubt," he wrote to a New York City paper, *The Observer*, "it will easily support a million of people."

Todd sent accounts of his annual Long Lake trips to *The Observer* each fall, but in October, 1844, one Joel T. Headley wrote to the same paper that, although he commended Todd for vacationing in the woods and for recommending that others do so, he questioned the agricultural future of a place like Long Lake. "When it comes to how many bushels of wheat it will yield to the acre," warned Headley, "it becomes quite another thing . . . . Indeed, we doubt whether this region will ever be much settled, until our western territory is all occupied."

Within a week Todd rejoined by raising the scientifically questionable point that once the forests were cut down, the climate of the central Adirondacks would moderate sufficiently to improve its prospects for agriculture. The following year, 1845, Todd's accounts were gathered into a little book called *Long Lake* which was published at Pittsfield, but by then it appeared that he was having second thoughts. He admitted to Headley that at Long Lake "the best people are all going away . . . . It won't be settled for a century." Headley confirmed to *The Observer* the following year that some of Long Lake's settlers had indeed moved out, that the church had failed, and that *"Not a man here supports himself from his farm"* (his emphasis). Most of the money in circulation there, he noted, came from state funds earmarked for road-building purposes. It was time, Headley said, to do away with "the romance of dreamers and the falsehoods of land speculators."

During the 1840s, Headley, like Todd, published some of his accounts in various New York newspapers. In 1849, he collected them with supplementary materials into a book that would remain the principal and most popular account of the region for the next twenty years. It was called *The Adirondack; or, Life in the Woods.* Headley dedicated his book to H. J. Raymond, who within a year or two would establish the *New York Daily Times* and himself was to make a trip to the Adirondacks in 1855 in support of the proposed Sacketts Harbor and Saratoga Railroad. Headley had been instrumental in helping to force a bill through the legislature in 1848 which granted this company extensive rights to land across the heart of the Adirondacks.

Raymond was among those who continued to believe that "the next ten years . . . will see this wilderness . . . filled with the life and energy of civilizing conquest," but most visitors in this period approached the Adirondacks on Headley's less ambitious terms. He extolled the simple outdoors and sporting life. "With a good pair of legs under you," he wrote, "a spirit not easily discouraged, and a love for the wild, and free, you can have a glorious tramp — enjoy magnificent scenery — catch a trout and kill deer to your heart's content, and come back to civilized life a healthier and a better man."

This too was the approach taken by the English-born painter Arthur Fitzwilliam Tait, who had come to the United States in 1850. Within a few years he had discovered the Adirondacks, painted there most summers, and depicted its woods, its game, and especially the activities of its sportsmen. Many of his works were published in hand-colored lithographs by Currier and Ives.

This too was the approach of the Philosophers — Ralph Waldo Emerson, Louis Agassiz, James Stillman and others from Concord and Boston — when they visited Follansbee Pond the summer of 1857. Stillman captured some of their activities on canvas; Emerson wrote a poem about their life in the woods; and, as Paul Jamieson points out in the second edition of his *Adirondack Reader,* Henry David Thoreau, in learning from Emerson on his return to Concord that the party had "broken some dozens of ale-bottles, one after another, with their bullets, in Adirondack country, using them for marks!" commented testily that "It sounds rather Cockneyish."

If visits to the woods had grown considerably during this period, as had books, articles, and paintings depicting these visits, it is remarkable how few people seemed to feel the need to do anything about the resources that made the visits and the enjoyments they yielded possible. Perhaps the danger of losing the resources simply was not apparent. There was talk of building railroads, but railroads weren't built. There was concern about logging and forest fires, but relatively little logging activity actually had penetrated the central Adirondacks.

An exception to this indifference was provided by an Albany newspaper editor named Samuel H. Hammond, whose views, though prophetic, probably did not exert a significant influence when his *Wild Northern Scenes* appeared in 1857. Floating down the Raquette River "on its tortuous and winding way for a hundred or more miles through an unbroken forest," he wrote, "with all the old things standing in their primeval grandeur along its banks," where "the woodsman's axe had not marred the loveliness of its surroundings," and where "no human hand has for all that distance . . . harnessed it to the great wheel, making it a slave, compelling it to be utilitarian," Hammond was inspired to suggest that "Had I my way, I would mark out a circle of a hundred miles in diameter, and throw around it

*Joel T. Headley's book **The Adirondack: Or, Life in the Woods**, published in 1849, featured many illustrations, among them this steel engraving of a sketch of Lake Colden done by Charles C. Ingham.*
Credit: William K. Verner

the protecting aegis of the constitution. I would make it a forest forever.... There is room enough for civilization in regions better fitted for it. I would consecrate these old forests, these rivers and lakes, these mountains and valleys to the Vagabond Spirit, and make them a place wherein a man could turn savage and rest, for a fortnight or a month, from the toils and cares of life."

The intervention of the Civil War gave the integral wilderness of the central Adirondacks a few more years of respite from civilized encroachments. The Philosophers did not return after 1859. Building of railroads was delayed for the war's duration. Some visitors continued to come to the Adirondacks, even during the war years, and, indeed, native moose became extinct the summer of 1862 at Raquette Lake, where Tait painted his popular camping scene "A Good Time Coming."

The Gilded Age

In the twenty years following the close of the Civil War, however, some important influences would come from developments far outside the region itself. On April 1, 1858, Frederick Law Olmsted and Calvert Vaux submitted a proposal called "Greensward" to New York City's Board of Commissioners of the Central Park. Olmsted and Vaux soon learned that their plan had been chosen over those of thirty-two competitors for the conversion of some 840 acres of pig farms, squatters' hovels, bone-boiling works, and sawmills into park land for the city. Six years later, in May, 1864, appeared a book called *Man and Nature;* its author was Vermonter George Perkins Marsh, who had spent many years overseas in the diplomatic service. In his book, Marsh surveyed the historical impact of human activity upon the natural environment in many parts of the world, and he offered suggestions for the maintenance of a sound balance between the works of man and the nature essential to his being. Speaking specifically of northern New York, he argued that the region could be protected in such a way that both "economical" factors such as watershed protection and future timber growth and "poetical" purposes such as the study of nature could be served.

Four months later, in August, 1864, taking a cue from the work of Olmsted and Vaux, a *New York Times* editorial noted the potential of a veritable "Central Park for the world" as it reported upon the beginning of work on Dr. Thomas C. Durant's Adirondack Railroad. Following up on another cue, this time quite possibly from Marsh's book, the editorialist suggested that not only would the railroad make the Adirondacks far more accessible than heretofore and open up its timber and mineral resources to the point where "the furnaces of our capitalists will line its valleys," but also that it would enable the visitor to find himself readily "in solitude almost as complete as when the 'Deerslayer' stalked his game in its fastnesses." Here too was a prime opportunity for "those of our citizens who desire to advance civilization by combining taste with luxury" to form "combinations" and seize "upon the choicest of the Adirondack Mountains" and make of them "grand parks, owned in common" where "they can enjoy equal amplitude and privacy of sporting, riding and driving, whenever they are able."

Meanwhile, Olmsted, having served on a health agency for part of the Civil War, had left New York and found himself managing a large private estate in

California beginning in the fall of 1863. He soon became associated with prominent San Franciscans interested in the protection of the Yosemite region and, by March of 1864, had helped lobby a bill through Congress to set the area aside "for public use, resort, and recreation for all time." Passed by both houses, the bill was signed by President Lincoln on June 30, 1864.

An external factor that may well have had an impact on the Adirondacks and on some of the people instrumental in its preservation was the publication in 1865 of Francis Parkman's *Pioneers of France in the New World*, the first in a series of seven books on "France and England in North America." Through the careful exploitation of primary resources, brilliant literary style, and widespread distribution, Parkman helped instill in the minds of his readers memorable images of what the vast American wilderness once had been and of the role it had played in the distinctive heritage of North America.

These predominantly external factors aside for a moment, dramatic changes within the Adirondack region itself were taking place in the years immediately following the Civil War. Because they have been so well documented elsewhere, it may be sufficient to note that, besides Dr. Durant's railroad, which reached North Creek in 1871, other railroads spread around and into the Adirondacks during this period. Steamboats appeared on many Adirondack lakes, and near Glens Falls in the late 1860s processes were refined for the conversion of softwoods into pulp and then into paper. This development promised the subjugation to logging of smaller diameter softwood trees than had hitherto been the case, and the coming of the railroads meant that hardwoods, which, because they do not float, had been spared from the lumberman's axe in earlier years, would lose their immunity as well.

Twenty years after the publication of Headley's book appeared *Adventures in the Wilderness; or, Camp-Life in the Adirondacks* by the Reverend W. H. H. Murray. This book and the phenomenal public reaction to it, both positive and negative, contributed to a veritable explosion of visitation to the region in the summer of 1869 and in years thereafter. Guidebooks by the likes of E. R. Wallace and S. R. Stoddard soon followed. Hotels to accommodate the onslaught sprang up, sometimes in places where before there had been no development whatsoever. As loggers moved deeper into the Adirondacks, seeking forest lands to cut, so too did wealthy individuals and groups seeking lands to establish private estates or clubs where they could build often elaborately rustic camps to house their families for summer vacations.

Observers made note of these dramatic changes at the time, but most were not at all clear as to what, if anything, should be done about them. Headley, as early as the 1869 expansion of his book, was of the opinion that "the change was not in the wilderness, but in the multitude and class of people that thronged it." Early in 1872, Murray, who perhaps unwittingly had contributed to the changes as much as anyone, was bemoaning the fact that the Adirondack region was "now ruined for the lover of solitude and nature . . . , the work of literary tourists and stage lines." Parkman, although not until shortly before his death in 1893, complained about what had become of the Lake George where he had camped a half century before. "The nouveau riche, who is one of the pests of this country," he wrote to a friend, "has now got possession of the lake and its islands. For my part, I would gladly destroy all his works and restore Lake George to its native savagery."

Parkman, like Hammond and Marsh before him, would have liked to have done something about the situation, and, as the 1870s developed, a few others did as well, although the formulation of a politically acceptable solution was slow in coming. Certainly a key figure in the process was Verplanck Colvin, a surveyor and explorer who found ways of getting his observations and illustrations before the public through the medium of print. Clearly under the influence of Marsh, and possibly under that of Parkman, and at least indirectly under that of Olmsted, Colvin made it known that the Adirondacks ought to be protected, combining the rationales of utility and enjoyment. Colvin's thoughts on the specific geographic and political focus of his concerns shifted about during the 1870s as he occupied himself with a state-sponsored survey of the Adirondacks. In 1874, he recommended beginning with an area of just under 400,000 acres in the High Peaks region and making this into a "park or timber reserve."

Headley, in updating his book again in 1875, made favorable note of the Colvin surveys but resisted the idea of legal "protection from the State"; rather, he offered the novel idea that, if the state simply bought up undeveloped railroad rights of way (including, presumably, what remained of the one he had lobbied for in 1848) and stopped passing on non-resident land tax revenues for the building of roads, "the forest will remain, practically, what it is forever."

That it would eventually come down to a matter of law, at least for state-owned lands, was indeed to be the case, but even the first more or less concrete step in that direction was only halting at best. On March 1, 1872, President Ulysses S. Grant signed into law the bill that nationalized Yellowstone "as a public park or pleasuring ground for the enjoyment and benefit of the poeple." Exactly two weeks later, the New York State legislature passed a bill creating a "Commission of State Parks" that was directed to look into the Adirondacks in particular. Colvin was a member of the commission, as was Franklin B. Hough, historian, statistician, and early proponent of a professional approach to forestry in America. Former Governor Horatio Seymour, who had guided a Lady-in-Waiting to Queen Victoria through the Adirondacks in 1855, was named chairman.

In reporting to the governor a year after its creation, the commission recognized the watershed, recreational, and health values of the Adirondacks and expressed concern about the impact of mining, tanning, lumbering, and fires upon the region. It warned that "protection of a great portion of that forest from wanton destruction is absolutely and immediately required" but was less clear as to just what steps should be taken to achieve this. As it was, for reasons undoubtedly political as well as circumstantial, nothing much was done. The new and often conflicting forces that had come upon the Adirondack scene in recent years proceeded in playing out their roles. One such development is reminiscent in kind of something that took place a hundred years later in the Adirondacks — the sudden reduction in second home project pressure, not because of land use and intensity guidelines of the newly created Adirondack Park Agency but rather because of widespread national economic recession. In the case of the decade between 1873, when the Parks commissioners had recorded approximately 40,000 Adirondack acres in public ownership, and 1883, when such holdings had grown to some 700,000 acres, it was not state action which had brought about this nearly eighteen-fold increase but rather landowners, lumbermen in particular, letting their lands go for unpaid taxes once they were finished with them.

By the early 1880s, interest in doing something concrete about the Adirondacks, or at least its state lands, arose yet again. Oddly enough, the specific reasons for this new interest have not been thoroughly documented. It may be assumed, however, that time had allowed civic groups, politicians, professionals, and the public at large to recognize more fully the negative impacts of indiscriminate logging and forest fires and to refine their appreciation for some of those positive, if often intangible, Adirondack qualities that were being lost. It may also have been that time was needed for the many newcomers to the Adirondack scene — transient vacationers and landowners — to consolidate their views as to what they wanted of the region.

As we have already suggested, the 1885 law that established the Forest Preserve was, in many respects, but a tentative step. It would not be for some years — decades, in fact — that "forever wild" came to be viewed by many as a wilderness preservation mandate pure and simple rather than as a means, *through* preservation, to conserve watershed and, perhaps, to assure a future timber supply. Wilderness as an end in itself (although more precisely a means towards achieving specialized recreational and historic preservation ends for human society) was a concept that would have to await public appreciation that, indeed, the American frontier was, for all practical purposes, no more (something the federal Census Bureau had announced in 1890). And it would have to await the emergence (as was the case with the creation of the Wilderness Society in 1935) of groups "of spirited people" who, in the words of Robert Marshall, "will fight for the freedom of the wilderness" through political action.

Whatever the precise reasons, the state in 1883 prohibited further sales of state-owned lands in ten of its northern counties, allocated $10,000 towards clearing up joint and disputed land titles, and instructed Colvin to begin a detailed survey of state holdings. Meanwhile, members of the new and growing American forestry profession began to organize, as did civic groups concerned about the future of the Adirondacks. In 1884, Charles Sprague Sargent of Harvard University was appointed by the state controller to study the Adirondacks and report back to him by the next legislative session. On January 23, 1885, Sargent submitted his report. The commissioners had visited the Adirondacks the previous summer, and, based in part on what they had seen there, they reported that the plundering of the forests "reduces this whole region to an unproductive and dangerous desert." They recognized the host of utilitarian and recreational factors that had to be taken into account in the Adirondacks, but, as a beginning, the existing state land in the northern New York counties had to be addressed, and the way to do that was to constitute these lands as a "forest preserve" and mandate that they "be forever kept as wild forest lands."

Following the submission of the Sargent Commission recommendations, other parties had opportunities to offer suggestions as well. Franklin B. Hough favored the creation of a forest *reserve* to be managed for its timber potential rather than a *preserve*, whose passive management, though it might be beneficial for watershed and limited recreational purposes, would defer active forest management. The German-born forester B. E. Fernow is said to have contributed specifics to the law ultimately adopted, although presumably these had to do with details of management and did not have bearing on the "forever wild" concept that had been introduced by the Sargent group. Politically, committees of the New York Board of Trade and Transportation and the Brooklyn Constitution Club played important roles behind the scenes in consolidating separate legislative bills into one, in refining the language to be employed, and in maintaining the pressure necessary to keeping the forest preserve idea alive before members of the legislature.

The press also did its part. Much as Eliot Porter's distinctive color photographs in his *Forever Wild: the Adirondacks* raised a later public's visual consciousness of the Adirondacks shortly before the Adirondack Mountains National Park proposal of 1967 — a concept which led directly to the creation of the Temporary Study Commission on the Future of the Adirondacks and the formation in 1971 of the Adirondack Park Agency — so must pictorial features, especially in *Harper's Weekly* during the winter of 1884-1885, have reminded an earlier public of problems in the Adirondacks. The front cover of the December 6, 1884, issue featured two panels based on drawings by Julian Rix of "Destruction of Forests in the Adirondacks," and additional pictures appeared inside. On January 24, 1885, two further Rix panels illustrated a short article by Sargent on "Forest Destruction," and the February 28 issue featured a full-page engraving by Daniel Beard on "Evicted Tenants of the Adirondacks," which depicted extirpated mammals of the region.

On May 11, 1885, the legislature completed passage of the forest preserve bill, and four days later Governor David B. Hill signed the measure into law. "Forever wild" had become established in New York State legal parlance and affixed to the Adirondacks and Catskills, or parts of them at least, for the years to come. In less than ten years, in fact, the phrase would enter the lexicon of the state constitution.

Romanticism, Wilderness, and Conservation

PHILIP G. TERRIE

On the 23rd of September, 1837, a remarkable series of letters began appearing in the *New York Mirror.* Written by Charles Fenno Hoffman — journalist, poet, novelist — these epistles captured the charm and grandeur of the central Adirondacks. Hoffman had read about the explorations of the New York Natural History Survey, which was bringing the first significant public attention to the vast wilderness of forests, lakes, and peaks west of Lake Champlain and which on August 5, 1837, had made the first recorded ascent of New York's highest mountain. Despite the encumbrance of a wooden leg, Hoffman wanted to see this wilderness for himself. And see it he did: he camped out in Indian Pass (where he and his companions were chilled by an early snowstorm), hiked in the vicinity of lakes Sanford and Henderson, and made a valiant effort to climb Marcy, thwarted only by that wooden leg.

Hoffman's interest in the Adirondacks reflected an important shift in American attitudes toward nature, and his trip to the wilderness of the High Peaks and Indian Pass represents the arrival in the region of an intriguing and influential figure — the romantic writer. Hoffman and the many romantics who followed him responded to the wilderness in ways radically different from those of earlier generations. Most Americans of the eighteenth century would have seen little allure in a landscape characterized mainly by mountains, trees, and wild animals. For them the only reason to be interested in land was economic; thus Sir William Johnson wrote of the southern Adirondacks in 1770 that the terrain was "so verry [sic] mountainous and barren that it is worth nothing." According to this line of thinking, land deserved attention only to the extent that it could be farmed or otherwise exploited and made to return a profit. Such views were typical of the day (and of course still enjoy considerable currency).

But Hoffman was not interested in speculating in real estate, in farming, or in buying shares in the struggling iron mine near Sanford Lake. He came to camp out, to admire the scenery, to spend time with the rustic hunter and guide John Cheney. Most important, he came to the wilderness because he thought it would be both entertaining and morally and spiritually edifying. By thus acknowledging such non-utilitarian possibilities in nature, Hoffman showed how the romantic movement was reshaping American culture.

Emerging in Europe in the middle of the eighteenth century, romanticism was a loose collection of ideas about mankind, the world, and God. European intellectuals reacted against what they thought was the cold, spiritless, mechanistic conception of reality common in the Enlightenment or Age of Reason. Among other things, they discovered in nature a spiritual warmth, and in nature, they believed, fallen modern man would find redemption. In the United States an additional precept developed: Americans believed that the grandness and purity of their wilderness would supply to their culture what centuries of history provided in Europe. In the early years of the Republic, Americans felt apprehensive about the quality of their literature and art; they feared lest the absence of castles, ruins, and all the paraphernalia of an aristocratic past would mean that the New World would never produce great poems, novels, and paintings. The cure for this sense of cultural inferiority was the spectacular American landscape itself. Europe had its history; we had our wilderness, which woūld be both the inspiration and subject of a new literature and art. The American wilderness, therefore, was expected by those intellectuals sensitive to cultural currents to be both spiritually redemptive and a source of patriotic pride.

By the early decades of the nineteenth century, Americans like Hoffman had absorbed fully the tenets of romanticism. And what Hoffman found in the Adirondacks satisfied him entirely. The letters that Hoffman dispatched to the *Mirror* (which were subsequently reprinted in the book *Wild Scenes in the Forest and Prairie*) became the first of hundreds of romantic responses to the glories of the Adirondack wilderness. Throughout the nineteenth century, educated, literate men — and a few women — camped and traveled in the Adirondacks and returned home to write descriptive articles and books about their adventures. Such documents, which eventually constituted a virtually distinct genre, helped to establish a public image of the Adirondacks as a special place. Invoking the romantic faith in the value of pristine nature, they encouraged throngs of Easterners to visit the region, and they painted a picture of a divine landscape. Thus, when at the end of the century lumbermen threatened the landscape, a public interested in protecting at least some of it was ready to defend the Adirondacks against forces inimical to the spiritual and aesthetic values of the wilderness.

One of the most important features of the wilderness was its scenic magnificence, and gushing reactions to scenery were essential to the romantic account of the wonders of the Adirondacks. Even from the otherwise skeptical pen of Thomas Bangs Thorpe, the Southwestern humorist, the Adirondacks elicited a positive response. After a camping trip up the Fulton chain, Thorpe wrote, "I question if there is in the wide world a place where the natural beauty so strongly combines every possible variety of expression to gratify the eye and call forth admiration." And John Todd, a Massachusetts minister who paid several visits to Long Lake in the 1840s, predicted that the marvels of the Adirondack landscape would soon make the region a popular resort: "The scenery on these lakes is grand and beautiful beyond anything of which I ever conceived. The lakes of Scotland have been celebrated of old in story and song; but the time will come, I doubt not, when these lakes will become the most interesting resort to be found in the country."

Two types of scenery especially appealed to romantic tourists. These were the rugged, spectacular terrain of the High Peaks and Indian Pass, characteristically referred to in the vocabulary of the day as "sublime," and the rolling, gentle, less imposing country around the central lakes, typically described as "beautiful." The inclination to classify types of landscape reflected the influence of a treatise on aesthetics by Edmund Burke, the English philosopher and historian. Joel T. Headley, whose 1849 volume *The Adirondack; Or Life in the Woods* was one of the most popular and most representative of romantic responses to the Adirondacks, observed these distinctions carefully. His description of the view from Mount Marcy, which he climbed sometime in the 1840s, emphasizes the

The Adirondack (or Indian) Pass has always been one of the most popular destinations for seekers of sublime scenery. This engraving, based on a painting by Charles C. Ingham, appeared in Joel T. Headley's The Adirondack, Or, Life in the Woods, *a widely circulating travel narrative first published in 1849 and reprinted by Harbor Hill Books in 1982. Credit: Harbor Hill Books,* The Adirondack supposedly frightening, overwhelming features of the sublime landscape: standing on the summit, Headley found himself "in the centre of a chaos of mountains, . . . all was grey, or green, or black, as far as the vision could extend. . .grand and gloomy. . .a background of mountains with nothing but the most savage scenery between — how mysterious — how awful it seemed." Despite the apparently negative characteristics of such terrain, romantics enthusiastically sought such locales, finding there a confirmation of the omnipotence of the Creator and the unique grandeur of the American wilderness.

Headley used a different vocabulary to describe the soothing tranquility he found at Forked Lake:

> All was wild but beautiful. The sun was stooping to the western mountains, whose sea of summits were calmly sleeping against the golden heavens: the cool breeze stirred a world of foliage on our right — green islands, beautiful as Elysian fields, rose out of the water as we advanced; the sparkling waves rolled as merrily under as bright a sky as ever bent over the earth, and for a moment I seemed to have been transported into a new world. I never was more struck by a scene in my life: its utter wildness, spread out there where the axe of civilization had never struck a blow —the evening — the sunset — the deep purple of the mountains — the silence and solitude of the shores, and the cry of the birds in the distance, combined to render it one of enchantment to me.

The notion that such intimacy with nature could leave one feeling "transported into a new world" was common among romantics, especially among the Concord-Cambridge intellectuals known as the transcendentalists. The acknowledged leader of this group, Ralph Waldo Emerson, visited the Adirondacks with several of his Massachusetts friends on a famous camping trip at Follansbee (now usually spelled Follensby) Pond in 1858. In a long blank-verse poem Emerson described the capacity of the wilderness to lead the individual consciousness to new and transcendent insights:

> Nature spoke
> To each apart, lifting her lovely shows
> To spiritual lessons pointed home,
> And as through dreams in watches of the night,
> So through all creatures in their form and ways
> Some mystic hint accosts the vigilant,
> Not clearly voiced, but waking a new sense
> Inviting to new knowledge, one with old.

The key to Emerson's discovery of this transcendence was his belief in the spiritual power of the landscape itself. It was a common article of the romantic faith that nature itself was divine, that, in fact, the landscape was sacred, and that God dwelt in nature. This belief in the immanence of God in nature is usually called pantheism. It appears, in one form or another, in nearly every Adirondack romantic travel narrative, often combined with the notion that nature is God's temple. For example, Benson J. Lossing, popular historian and author of a book describing the entire route of the Hudson from its Adirondack sources to the Atlantic, thus described his first Sunday in the wilderness:

> It was a perfect summer day, and all around us were freshness and beauty. We were alone with God and His works, far away from the abodes of men; and when at evening the stars came out one by one, they seemed hung up in the dome of a great cathedral, in which we had that day worshipped so purely and lovingly.

Likewise, Alfred Billings Street, who wrote two books about the Adirondacks and after whom Street Mountain near Heart Lake is named, affirmed that in the wilderness one is more likely to commune with God. He employed the metaphor of the forest as temple:

> The wilderness is one great tongue, speaking constantly to our hearts; inciting to knowledge of ourselves and to the love of the Supreme Maker, Benefactor, Father . . . Here, with the grand forest for our worshipping temple, our hearts expanding, our thoughts riding unfettered, we behold Him, face to face.

Even when romantic travelers were not overtly religious in their appreciation of the wilderness, they found many reasons to be positive about the wilderness experience. A common theme in romantic narratives was the conviction that in the wilderness one is free in a way impossible in towns and cities. As Headley put it,

> In the woods, the mask that society compels one to wear is cast aside, and the restraints which the thousand eyes and reckless tongues about him fasten on the heart are thrown off, and the soul rejoices in its liberty and again becomes a child in action . . . How the soul awakes in this new existence, and casting off the fetters that has [sic] bound it, rejoices in broader liberty, and leaps with a new exultant feeling . . . Oh! how I love the glorious woods and the sense of freedom they bring.

The scholars with Emerson also felt their youth restored and their responsibilities lifted:

> They fancied the light air
> That circled freshly in their forest dress
> Made them to boys again. Happier that they
> Slipped off their pack of duties, leagues behind,
> At the first mounting of the giant stairs.

No placard on these rocks warned to the polls,
No door-bell heralded a visitor.
No courier waits, no letter came or went.
Nothing was ploughed, or reaped, or bought, or sold.

As these writers considered the spirituality of the wilderness as well as its capacity to supply freedom and escape from an increasingly complex and urban America, some of them noticed how rare wilderness was becoming. At the beginning of the era of the romantic traveler, Hoffman had acknowledged that what he found in the Adirondacks existed nowhere else in New York State. "It seems strange," he wrote, "to find so wild a district in 'one of the old thirteen,' the empire state of New York." Street expressed his awareness of this in verse:

And now behold our noble Empire State!
The wilderness hath vanished like a curl
From nature's brow, save where the grand peaks
Of the stern Adirondach [*sic*] challenge heaven,
And mid whose solemn forests, lakes stretch out
Their silver shields, and ponds their sparkling eyes,
And brooks their branching veins; where wanders still
The mighty moose, and by his shaded stream
The beaver lingers; region wild and rude!

But it was hard for romantics to move from an awareness of both the virtues and rareness of wilderness to an overt call for its preservation. Most writers, while convinced of the beneficence of nature in all its forms, were also susceptible to other, peculiarly American romantic themes: these included an often jingoistic faith in the mission of the American people to carry civilization from sea to shining sea and a profound trust in the abstract notion of progress. Both of these doctrines are antithetical to the preservation of wilderness. Thus most romantics were caught in an irreconcilable dilemma. They found the wilderness appealing both because their culture insisted that all of nature was virtuous and because their own experience in the wilderness was generally positive. As forward-looking Americans, however, they felt that the greatness of their country depended on the continuing evolution of the continent away from wilderness and toward utility, progress, productivity.

Many romantics in the Adirondacks seemed unconsciously aware of this paradox. While unable to declare outright that the wilderness ought to be preserved for future generations, they emphasized all the positive features of the wilderness and either ignored or mildly regretted what would inevitably happen to it in the future. A few others, most notably Samuel H. Hammond, an Albany journalist, called for outright protection. Hammond's arrival at this position was halting: in the first of two books he wrote about camping in the Adirondack wilderness (*Hills, Lakes and Forest Streams,* 1854) he was able only to hint at the need for preservation. And he expressed even this tentative declaration not in his own narrative voice but in that of his guide:

It's only the rocky and barren nater [sic] of the country around us, that saves this wild region from what I call the desolation of civilization, and the mighty changes it works on the face of a country; and I'm glad it's so. There should be left, some broad sweep of wild woods, where a man can get free of the sights and sounds of the clearin's, and look upon nater, as it came from the hands of the great Creator, with all the wild animals, and nateral things that belonged to it in the times of old.

In *Wild Northern Scenes,* published three years later, Hammond put his distaste for the encroachments of civilization in his own voice and suggested that the Adirondacks could be saved forever. His plea for preservation is an example of another paradoxical feature of romanticism: anti-modernism, a distrust, usually only implicit, of the direction of modern civilization. For many people — even some who ostensibly approved of progress and industrialism — it was precisely such doubts about the values of a modern, commercial, utilitarian world that led them to the wilderness in the first place. And they also realized that the wilderness was particularly threatened by the commercial mind. Praising the glories of the wilderness, Hammond decried "worldliness, greed for progress, thirst for gain" and detested the mentality which believed that "everything in the heavens, or on the earth, or in the waters, were [sic] to be measured by the dollar and cent standard, and unless reducible to a representative of moneyed value, to be thrown, as utterly worthless, away."

In a crucial and, for its time radical, statement Hammond worried about what life would be like if wilderness in the Adirondacks were eliminated, and asked,

When that time shall have arrived, where shall we go to find the woods, the wild things, the old forests, and hear the sounds which belong to nature in its primeval state? Whither shall we flee from civilization, to take off the harness and be free, for a season, from the restraints, the conventionalities of society, and rest from the cares and toils, the strifes and competitions of life? Had I my way, I would mark out a circle of a hundred miles in diameter, and throw around it the protecting aegis of the constitution. I would make it a forest forever. It should be a misdemeanor to chop down a tree, and a felony to clear an acre within its boundaries. The old woods should stand here always as God made them, growing on until the earthworm ate away their roots, and the strong winds hurled them to the ground, and new woods should be permitted to supply the place of the old so long as the earth remained. There is room enough for civilization in regions better fitted for it. It has no business among these mountains, these rivers and lakes, these gigantic boulders, these tangled valleys and dark mountain gorges. Let it go where labor will garner a richer harvest, and industry reap a better reward for its toil. It will be of stinted growth at best here.

Alone among romantic writers Hammond issued a call for absolute preservation: he foresaw a landscape protected much as the Forest Preserve is today, with no utilitarian interference in the environment. He hoped that the Adirondack wilderness could be saved for its spiritual value, for the benefits it offered to the often jaded spirit of modern man. Although other romantics were not willing to go so far as Hammond did in insisting on the importance of wilderness, all of them helped prepare the popular consciousness for the preservation steps taken in 1885 and 1894. Those steps largely reflected practical concerns — fears about the deteriorating Adirondack watershed. But the popular conviction that the Adirondacks were a special place, a region to be treasured for other than utilitarian reasons, was important in assuring public acceptance of any statutory protection. In the twentieth century this sense of the Adirondacks as uniquely valuable has exercised an increasing power in guaranteeing that the wilderness remains preserved.

"Men To Match My Mountains . . ."

WARDER H. CADBURY

The program committee of the Troy Lyceum had invited Farrand N. Benedict, retired professor from the University of Vermont, to give a public evening lecture on a topic of his own choice. The year was 1872, and the legislature of the State of New York had appointed a special commission, with the young Verplanck Colvin as its secretary, to consider making the Adirondacks a "public park," and had authorized the first topographical survey of the region under Colvin's direction.

As he considered the subject, Benedict's first inclination for his talk was to tell the story of his ascent of Mt. Marcy many years earlier in 1839 to measure the exact altitude of this highest peak in the state. Unfortunately, he finally persuaded himself to give instead a discourse on mountains in general. As a consequence of this characteristic modesty Benedict's pioneering role at the very beginning of Adirondack history has remained largely untold.

Together with Ebenezer Emmons, a better known contemporary and early explorer of the Adirondacks, Benedict's career spanned the decades of America's growth as a robust agricultural and industrial nation. A proud and patriotic poet, Samuel Walter Foss, caught the spirit of the times in this verse:

> Bring me men to match my mountains,
> Bring me men to match my plains,
> Men with empires in their purpose
> And new eras in their brains.

One hundred and fifty years ago the Adirondack region was fortunate to have had men such as Benedict and Emmons to match its mountains, for both cherished imperial visions of its promising future. The celebration of the centennial of the Forest Preserve in 1985 is thus an appropriate occasion to do two things: to document and honor, at last, Benedict's achievements, and to show how he and his friend Emmons helped set in motion both events and ideas that eventually evolved into the establishment of the largest wilderness park in the country.

Farrand Benedict, at the age of 30 and newly married, came in 1833 to the University of Vermont as professor of mathematics and civil engineering. In addition to a fine education from Hamilton College, he brought with him a special extracurricular talent, what the quaint language of the nineteenth century called "a great partiality for pedestrian tours." In short, he was something of a backpacker long before the recreation became as widely popular as it is today.

From the college campus at Burlington, the Adirondacks were clearly visible across the gleaming waters of Lake Champlain, but at that time the mountains were unmeasured, unmapped and unknown. It was a friend and prominent businessman, William Coventry H. Waddell, who suggested to Benedict "the expediency of his pursuing his rambles in the northern part of New York, and stated as a provocative to research that [he] had never been able to find a man who had crossed the wilderness [from one side to the other]." This challenge fired Benedict's imagination, and he at once became the first scientific explorer to visit the region.

It was 1835 when Benedict began the habit of spending a month's vacation each summer in the Adirondacks, partly for health and recreation. But he could not

Photo of Farrand N. Benedict
Credit: The Adirondack Museum, Blue Mountain Lake, NY

entirely shed his vocation as an engineer. While "traversing these forests," he wrote, "it has been my care, as far as convenient, during these tours, to inform myself of the soil, climate and business capabilities of the country."

From the start Benedict seems to have set his mind on the quest for an east-west passage through the wilderness straight across the Adirondack plateau, rather than content himself with shorter, circuitous and random excursions. By making local inquiries he found that settlers on the fringes of the mountains spoke of a "singular chain of waters" — rivers, lakes and ponds — that extended in a nearly uniform direction southwest from the opposite side of the lake, across from his front door in Burlington, towards the Erie Canal at Rome. He learned that

> Hunters have transported in small boats their treasures of fish, game and fur through these waters, from the vicinity of the settlements on Lake Champlain to the valley of the Black River. From their accounts it appeared that the "carrying places" were few and short, and that their voyages were accomplished without much labor or hazard.

"My own travels over this route," concluded Benedict, "which were commenced in 1835, verified these statements."

That date is noteworthy, for, by a coincidence that delights the historian, this year of the centennial of the Adirondack Forest Preserve is at the same time the sesquicentennial of the first exploration of the region by a professionally trained civil engineer and cartographer. Yet Benedict's name is nowhere on the map today to commemorate the man. Furthermore, he never got around to putting onto paper a narrative of these history-making excursions, so we are left with some tantalizing questions: what, for example, was the origin and design of those portable skiffs as antecedents of the later Adirondack guideboat, and what adventures did he encounter in traversing the wilderness?

We do know that Farrand Benedict's companion sometimes was his much younger brother Joel, who many years later wrote a brief account of their trips. In 1838, when "I was 17 years old," he began,

> I made a first visit with brother Farrand to a beautiful little valley near the foot of Whiteface Mountain. Here lived one of those interesting characters or frontiermen by the name of [Jacob?] Lobdell. He lived in a small log house on the back of a little brook that came directly from the base of the mountain, out of which my brother and myself have taken many a speckled trout . . . . The next year, 1839, Farrand and I again crossed from Burlington to Lobdell's and from there taking him as guide we went up the Saranac to old Capt. Miller's at the foot of Lower Saranac Lake.

The two brothers returned to the Adirondacks together each summer until Joel's last trip in 1843: "We went with [Amos] Hough [of Long Lake] through to Raquette Lake and beyond to the Eighth Lake on the Middle Branch of the Moose River, and thence to the Indian Plains on the South Branch of the Moose."

It was in 1837 when Professor Ebenezer Emmons, one of the most distinguished geologists in the country and associated with the Natural History Survey of New York, was the leader of an expedition which on August 5 made the first ascent of the highest mountain in the Adirondacks and state. Once they reached its rocky summit, and quite conscious of the fact that they were making history, the party promptly named the peak Mt. Marcy in honor of the governor. The five woodsmen who did the carrying and trailblazing included John Cheney and Harvey Holt, the first generation of Adirondack guides or mountain men.

While the details of this important occasion were well documented and are widely known today, it happened that measuring Mt. Marcy provoked an unexpected and somewhat unseemly controversy among the experts. In his report published the following year of 1838, Emmons officially proposed the name "Adirondacks" for these rugged mountains, and noted that his barometric observations gave Mt. Marcy an altitude of 5,487 feet above sea level. The very next year, however, in a report of a survey of a proposed railroad from Ogdensburg to Lake Champlain, the altitude was given as five hundred feet less. The author was Edwin F. Johnson, who later became one of the most distinguished railroad engineers in the country. To explain the "discrepancy" between his figure and that of Emmons, he noted that he used a trigonometric method, deducing the altitude from the angle of elevation to the summit observed from a point near Lake Champlain and Mt. Marcy's distance along a baseline as determined by a map.

Emmons seems to have taken offense at these brief remarks. So in his next annual report, dated February 1839, he noted that "it is quite doubtful whether the mountain in question [Marcy] is distinguishable from those of the same group," especially by a person who had never visited the High Peak region. Even if visible, he concluded, Johnson's measurement "is not entitled to consideration except as a very imperfect approximation."

The July 1839 issue of the prestigious *American Journal of Science* published a rejoinder by Johnson, arguing for the superior precision of trigonometric methods for determining the height of mountains. His conclusion was that "Mr. Emmons's barometric measurement of Mt. Marcy may be farther from the truth then he is willing to admit."

To put an end to this squabble, Emmons asked Benedict, who was recognized in the scientific community as impartial and highly qualified, to make a special ascent of Mt. Marcy for the purpose of obtaining more numerous and thorough observations in order to determine the true altitude to everyone's satisfaction. Benedict promptly agreed thus to arbitrate the dispute, at his own expense, and returned to the Adirondacks for a second visit that summer, but this time without his brother Joel. When he got home again, he wrote a long, technical account which Emmons published verbatim in his annual report early in 1840 and again in his final report in 1842.

With characteristic modesty, Benedict's paper was all business. Except for thanking his hosts at the village of the iron works, where an old blast furnace still stands, and "passing over every other personal circumstance connected with my ascent," Benedict's essay explained the mathematical computations required to translate his observations of air pressure and temperature into feet above sea level. It was not until many years later, in 1877, when Benedict finally told something of the story of his ascent of the mountain peak in a personal letter of condolence that was prompted by news of the death of his old guide.

My acquaintance with John Cheney began in the month of August, 1839 — 38 years ago. On Saturday, August 10, I arrived [at the mining village] as the guest of Mr. McIntyre. The next day (Sunday) I first became acquainted with John Cheney. On the next day (Monday) he piloted me to the Adirondack Pass. On the 13th we started from Lake Henderson for Mt. Marcy through the woods without path or blazed line. We camped that night on the edge or base of the naked rocky cone. At six o'clock the next morning, we were on the summit in a cold and piercing rain storm. John bundled me up in one or two Indian blankets and left me to my comfort in taking observations in the rain. In the meantime, he and Mr. George McRae, a young collegiate botanist, repaired to a sheltered spot on the south side of the peak.

Fortunately for Benedict, the rain and clouds began to dissipate in a couple of hours, and by ten o'clock in the morning, the sun came out. "In the afternoon," his letter continued, "we shambled down in double quick time over the ledges and stretched out that night . . . on the banks of Lake Colden. The next day (15th) we returned to the Upper Works in rather dilapidated condition. By this time John and I began to know each other. I was then 37 years old and he 40."

But what were Benedict's feelings as he stood alone on that rocky summit, the highest in the state, surrounded by an unbroken wilderness, and watched the stormy weather depart? Since others had recently published accounts of the Adirondacks, he remarked in his report only that "it would seem unnecessary for me to add that there are probably few places in North America where nature is invested with more magnificence and solitude than on these mountain peaks."

As an engineer, Benedict was simply not inclined to articulate literary and philosophical themes. But his first cousin, Joel T. Headley, who later became an important Adirondack author, put into his own words his recollections of a conversation with Benedict regarding this dramatic day on Mt. Marcy:

He ascended it once for scientific purposes, and made experiments on the top which have been of great service to the state. He said that the spectacle from it one morning in a northeast storm was sublime beyond description. *He* was in the clear sunlight, while an ocean of clouds rolled on below him in vast white undulations, blotting out the whole creation from his view.

At length, under the influence of the sun, this limitless deep slowly rent asunder, and the black top of a mountain emerged like an island from the mighty mass, and then another and another, till away, for more than three hundred miles in circumference, these black conical islands were sprinkled over the white bosom of the vapory sea. The lower portions of the mountains appeared, while the mist collected in the deep gulfs, and lay like a vast serpent over the bed of a river that wound through the forest below, or shot up into fantastic shapes, resembling towers and domes, and cliffs, and clouds, forming and shifting, and changing in bewildering confusion. It is impossible to conceive anything half so strange and wild.

It is noteworthy that Emmons experienced the same two contrasting responses to an identical situation on the stormy peak of Nippletop just two years earlier. On the one hand, he was anxious for the air to clear so he could get on with his surveying duties. On the other hand, he was powerfully moved by witnessing the drama of wind and fog. "It is difficult to say," he wrote, "whether our love of science or admiration of the intrinsic beauty and sublimity of the scene" was more dominant as he watched "the lifting up of the cloudy envelope from the neighboring summits, one after another, in the order of its elevation."

These pioneering mountain men thus shared a double vision of the Adirondacks. From the start, Americans have always viewed wilderness as something to conquer and to plunder of its natural riches. Yet, perhaps to their own surprise, Emmons and Benedict also experienced a new, non-materialistic appreciation of its worth to man as a source of health for body and soul. As the cultural historian Philip Terrie has recently observed, in the recesses of the Adirondack forests, on the summits of mountains they were the first to ascend, on the uninhabited shores of Adirondack lakes, these men perceived the joys of intimacy with untouched wilderness and asserted to a busy civilization the value of the spiritual forces immanent in wild nature.

The conflicting tensions between a utilitarian and a romantic view of nature were not evident to these first mountain men, perhaps because the region seemed vast enough for both to coexist side by side. But this very ambivalence towards the Adirondacks has from the start influenced popular attitudes and policy ever since. The contradictions slowly set in motion an historical dialectic from exploitation to recreation, and then to conservation and finally to the preservation of the wilderness whose centennial we are celebrating.

In occasional paragraphs scattered throughout his long scientific reports, Emmons was more articulate and lyrical than Benedict in going beyond mere narrative to testify to the spiritual dimensions of the Adirondacks wilderness, a land

> unrivalled for its magic and enchantment . . . . It is not by description that the scenery of this region can be made to pass before the eye of the imagination; it must be witnessed; the solitary summits in the distance, the cedars and firs which clothe the rock and shore, must be seen; the solitude must be felt . . . before all the truth in the scene can be realized. There are elements in the landscape, all of which are felt when there, but are lost in the words of a description, and untransferable by the pencil of the artist.

We know less of Benedict's feelings in response to the wilderness experience because, unfortunately, he wrote much less than Emmons, and his later survey reports were largely mathematical and technical. Furthermore, he may have felt it would be inappropriate for an engineer, or that he lacked the requisite literary skills. "Of the beauties of this unrivalled sheet of water," he wrote of Raquette Lake in 1874 as an old man, "I shall say nothing here. I leave this theme to the poet and the artist." But Benedict's track record is eloquent. In the twenty years following his first explorations in 1835, he spent at least a month in the Adirondacks each summer, partly, it must be noted, for business. He came to know the face of the land and its waterways more intimately than any of his peers. And he began because he was from the start a man who liked to rough it.

As a geologist, Emmons naturally focused on the potential wealth of the mineral, timber and agricultural resources. He estimated the iron ore at the mines at the foot of Mt. Marcy to be worth at least $300 million. While admitting that the climate on the high Adirondack plateau was cold and damp, he felt it could be easily improved by the simple expedient of cutting down all the trees, letting in the bright warm sunlight, and drying out the swampy bogs, "The axe has been laid at the foot of the tree," wrote Emmons in 1838 in a flight of poetic prophecy, "and ere long where naught now greets the eye, but a dense, and to appearance impassible forest, will be seen the golden grain waving with the gentle breeze, the sleek cattle browsing on the rich pastures, and the farmer with well stored granaries enjoying the domestic hearth."

In 1835, it will be recalled, Benedict had begun his Adirondack exploration as something of a lark, in response to a challenge to find a feasible route through the wilderness from one side to the other. A few years later, in 1840, as a postscript to his long report on measuring the altitude of Mt. Marcy, he added a few paragraphs regarding his discovery of the "remarkable fact" that the systems of rivers and lakes form an "almost unparalleled extent of natural batteau navigation." He estimated that by excavating some six miles for canals and building locks with a lift of 240 feet, the Saranac and Raquette Rivers would form a continuous water highway over 200 miles long.

This was the first serious and informed proposal published to open up the entire Adirondack plateau with a transportation network to encourage commercial development. Nothing came of it right away, but Benedict persistently returned to the region each summer to enlarge and expand his data. He later mentioned "the numerous and peculiar difficulties that crowd around an engineer in his progress through an unbroken wilderness."

The key to such dreams of empire was the absolute necessity for a transportation system to unlock the treasures of the Adirondacks and take them to market, and this goal became Benedict's ruling passion. The wilderness, noted a report in which he had a role, is "as completely shut off from all cultivation, all industry and improvement and all intercourse with the world as if it were ten thousand leagues, instead of fifty miles, from the seats of civilization and of active life. A region of the country larger than Vermont, equal to one fifth of the whole State, lies thus in the very heart of the State of New York, isolated, abandoned and desolate."

There must be no doubt, however, that in the minds of both of these mountain men it was the exploitive rather than the aesthetic or spiritual attitude towards the wilderness that commanded their energies. They were truly, as the poet put it, men with empires in their purpose and new eras in their brains. They were largely blind to the internal contradictions of a double vision for the region's future.

In 1845, Benedict was the obvious choice of a group of enterprising capitalists to survey and report in more detail upon a possible route for a combination of both railroad and slack-water navigation by steamboat from Port Kent on Lake Champlain to Boonville on the Black River Canal. Technical details aside, some of his comments in passing are shrewd observations. "The hunters, who long have practically held undisputed possession of the country, have had strong temptations so to represent it as to discourage settlement." Indeed, the hunter actually *sees* little of those wilds but the boggy acres for two reasons: the easiest, if not the only, mode of travel is by small boat along the "lines of natural navigation" of the rivers, and the "habits and instincts of the animals which he pursues" keep the deer and beaver close to the waterways. "The good and feasible [agricultural] land is almost universally concealed from the sight of the traveler" by the thick growth along the water's edge, "unless he takes the trouble to interrupt his journey and penetrate the woods on foot."

The most "fatal" obstacle to the colonization of the Adirondacks and exploitation of its natural resources remained the lack of transportation to market. This "paralyzes the efforts of the settler, and either forces him [to abandon the country] or compels him, however reluctant he may be, to follow the chase for articles of easier conveyance. Thus, furs are sought after instead of the bulkier products of the soil, and the farmer is gradually but surely transformed into the hunter."

But Benedict himself was anything but discouraged. The "beautiful and picturesque" lakes of the region, he wrote, "admired as they have been recently by travelers of taste . . . must ere long force themselves upon the attention of the businessman and the economist." What he did not say was that he was betting that the Adirondacks would indeed soon become a productive and profitable empire, and that he himself would cash in on its inevitable prosperity. He began to speculate in real estate.

"Forseeing that at some day or other," noted an article in the *New York Times*,

> which could not in the nature of things be very distant, [the Adirondacks] must come into notice, and knowing its intrinsic value, Professor Benedict selected various tracts which seemed to him most valuable, and bought them — part from individuals and part from the state; and as neither private owners nor the state officers knew anything whatever about the character of the lands, they parted with them at an absurdly low price, deeming themselves fortunate in being able to get anything for lands which they were inclined to consider valueless.

In the next decades, several trans-Adirondack railway schemes were proposed and incorporated, at least on paper, and most of them were based upon Benedict's pioneering surveys. His knowledge of the region's topography made it clear to him that no matter what particular route was finally selected, the central location of Raquette Lake made it the keystone to any transportation network. So Benedict acquired nearly all the thirty-six square miles that embrace its shores as Township 40. It was reported that, together with other members of his family, he came to own at one time or another close to 150,000 acres of Adirondack woods and waters.

Fortunately for the Forest Preserve of today, these dreams of empire in the Adirondacks were not realized at the time. The closing of the iron mines at Tahawus, competition from the Erie Canal and the lure of the flat farmlands of the Midwest, skepticism on the part of industrialists with the needed capital, the financial crisis of 1857, and then the Civil War all saved the wilderness from the ravages of progress. And the men who first publicized such dreams fell upon hard times. Ebenezer Emmons went south to become geologist for the state of North Carolina, where he died in 1863 amidst the maelstrom of the Civil War. About 1855, Farrand Benedict's wife became ill. In order to give her his constant personal care, he resigned from the University of Vermont, and they moved back to her family home in the more benign climate of New Jersey, while he turned most of his land speculation business over to relatives.

But the work of Emmons and Benedict in the Adirondacks had other important consequences than the failure of their dreams. The printed reports they authored attracted others to the wilderness for the first time, travelers and sportsmen who, in turn, publicized to the people of New York a quite different sort of vision for the region, a vision in which recreation and aesthetic satisfaction replaced economic exploitation.

When Emmons made the first ascent of Marcy in August of 1837, the party included Charles C. Ingham, a distinguished painter who provided some illustrations for the geologist's reports. In the following decades, nearly every important American landscape artist put the Adirondacks on his itinerary and his canvases. And when a young literary editor in Manhattan, Charles Fenno Hoffman, read in the newspapers about the mountain trip, he dropped his pen and headed north immediately. His published accounts of the beauties of the region attracted a wide audience, and the nickname "Tahawus" was coined. His prose portrait of the exploits of John Cheney, "mighty hunter of the Adirondacks," became a classic bit of local literature.

Benedict also influenced significant changes in the direction of Adirondack history. The commencement speaker at his University of Vermont in Burlington in 1841 was the Reverend John Todd, one of the most prominent clergymen in the nation. When this honored guest asked to accompany Benedict on his next excursion to the mountains, the professor could not very gracefully refuse. Todd returned to the Adirondacks for several summers, and published a little book called *Long Lake* which began to attract tourists to the mountains.

In 1844 Benedict suggested to his first cousin, Joel T. Headley, who was suffering from a nervous breakdown, that he go to the Adirondacks to mend his health. The cure worked, and Headley returned to the wilderness several summers over the next two decades. His book about his hunting and fishing adventures first appeared in 1849 and was enormously popular. Benedict contributed a short introduction to a new and enlarged edition in 1864.

So it happened that a scientist and an engineer, Emmons and Benedict, attracted to the Adirondacks the first generation of literary travelers whose writings soon drew increasing numbers of ordinary folk in pursuit of fish and game and outdoor recreation. And the very same trans-Adirondack chain of lakes and rivers, orginally surveyed by Benedict with grand visions of its agricultural and industrial potentials, became instead a convenient water route for sportsmen and their guides with their portable little rowboats.

After an absence from Adirondack affairs of nearly twenty years, Farrand Benedict returned in the 1870s following the death of his wife. In 1872, Verplanck Colvin placed the first theodolite on the summit of Mt. Marcy and made a computation of 5,333 feet above sea level. In 1875, Colvin measured it again, this time with a level and rod. The result was a bit higher, 5,344 feet, which is the same figure that Benedict had arrived at forty-six years earlier on that lonely, rainy morning.

At the request of the state legislature, in the summer of 1874 Benedict made yet another Adirondack survey of the waters of the upper Hudson and Raquette Rivers. But the purpose this time was not to cut the forests and build steamboat lines. Rather, it was to build reservoirs to conserve the precious supply of water so desperately needed for navigation on the Champlain Canal and Hudson River during the dry summer months. Still the engineer and scientist, he was close friends of the Chase family in Newcomb, and commissioned them to keep watch on a rain gauge so that more accurate data about the watershed would be possible.

In 1877, now an old man, Benedict learned of the death of John Cheney. Reminiscing briefly about his trip up Marcy with him many years before, he wrote:

> This was the only time he went with me as guide. Since then we have kept up a pleasant intimacy. I have always looked upon John as a necessary appendage to the Adirondacks, almost as necessary as Mt. Marcy itself. He has left a good name behind him — and this, [as the Biblical book of] Solomon says, is better than precious ointment.

Gateways to the Wilderness

J. ROBERT WILLIAMS

At a little after half past five on Wednesday afternoon, July 2, 1924, Miss Sadie Goodspeed, who lived nearby, saw flames coming out of the Forge House roof. Before the day was over, that proud and famous old caravansary at the foot of the first of the Fulton Chain of lakes in Old Forge was in ruins. The *Boonville Herald* reported in its next issue, "The entire village, men, women, and children alike, turned out *en masse* to fight the flames, strengthened by the village volunteer fire department and scores of men from Big Moose, Eagle Bay, Inlet, and Forestport, who rushed to the scene in speeding autos as news of the blaze spread throughout the countryside."

The fire was not an unusual event. Old, dry-timbered, clapboard-sided, shingle-roofed Adirondack hotels burned easily, with or without encouragement. One by one, the inns and boarding houses, as well as the splendid hotels of the elegant, turbulent, devil-take-the-hindmost Victorian Adirondacks would disappear, by fire, decay, demolition, or conversion to more profitable uses, even as harbingers of a new age aborning swarmed in "speeding autos," lickety-split over bumpy backwoods roads and wagon tracks in search of an elusive lotus land.

Just as the motorcar and its ubiquitous offshoots, the motel, the gas pump, and the fast food dispenser, were agents of social change in the Adirondacks, as elsewhere, in the twentieth century, so was the woodland hotel or boarding house both the symbol and the instrument of change in the nineteenth. E.R. Wallace's excellent *Descriptive Guide to the Adirondacks* for 1887 lists more than 200 establishments with almost 16,000 beds, all told; 267 hotels and boarding houses with 26,266 beds if Saratoga Springs, the Thousand Islands, and some towns around the Adirondack perimeter are counted. Wallace's list included only houses that could put up ten or more guests. Whether these hostelries were peaceful, restorative havens for contemplation, rest, and recreation, or staging grounds for rapacious assaults upon wilderness wildlife, especially deer and trout, is a good question. There is evidence both ways. And while the hotel business boomed, unbridled lumbering was tearing the heart out of this marvelous American treasure land. The time was surely, in that Gilded Age, growing ripe for reform.

It is hard to know when, or even whether, anything happens for the first time. Origins of long-term movements which redirect social custom and habit are dimly lit and easily ignored. Someone must have been the first to ask for and receive payment from a traveler for board and lodging in an Adirondack shelter, but who is to say who it was?

Indians, missionaries, soldiers, and beaver trappers whacked through the bush in the 1600s, but raised no settlements there worth notice. Colonists wanted arable land; they had trouble enough trying to farm it in New England without tackling the thin soil of a *terra incognita*. Nor was there interest in recreational deer shooting or trout fishing; no urge, either, to climb mountains for the fun of it.

Land speculators made Adirondack history in the eighteenth century. Totten and Crossfield, Macomb, Noble, Jessup, McCormick, Constable were names that would be identified with vast tracts, as millions of acres were bought and sold, often sight unseen. A few clusters of transplanted Vermonters hovered around the northeast fringe; settlers from the Mohawk Valley edged closer on the south. A man named Theophilus Anthony, from Manhattan, may or may not have built a camp beside a pond near Long Lake in 1786. Most Adirondack historians today doubt it.

John Brown of Providence, not the excitable abolitionist of Harper's Ferry and North Elba, but a rich Rhode Island merchant, had two sons-in-law. One, John Francis, was seduced by land dealers, Aaron Burr among them, into buying more than 200,000 wilderness acres, to this day known as the Brown's Tract. Another son-in-law, Charles Frederick Herreshoff, built a spacious manor house on the Tract and spent seven years trying to make the investment pay, having declared, "I will settle this tract, or it will settle me." He offered inducements to colonists, who came, but wouldn't stay. He tried iron mining and sheep farming, and went broke. Nothing turned out right for Herreshoff, and in 1819 he shot himself.

Next to occupy Herreshoff's house was Nat Foster, a famous guide and trapper, who leased it in 1832. Foster had shot seventy-six deer in one season, he kept a line of four hundred muskrat traps, and, some said, he could load and fire a flintlock musket six times in one minute. He carried spare bullets in loose skin pouches between his fingers, and he was double-jointed. Foster left the area in 1834 after his acquittal of the killing of the Indian Peter Waters, known as Drid.

In 1837, Otis Arnold moved into the Herreshoff manor with his wife and daughter, nucleus of a family which was to include a son and a dozen lively daughters, who raced horses bareback for the entertainment of passing wayfarers, and who built smudge fires under their cows at milking time, not to improve the quality of the milk, as they were inclined to tell onlookers, but to drive away punkies. As time passed, more and more people stopped at Arnold's for a meal or a bed for the night. Some of them wrote letters to friends and to newspapers in large cities about the primitive guest house and its interesting occupants until "Arnold's" came to be "a household word in Adirondack annals," as historian Alfred Donaldson observed. "It became probably the first house of entertainment in the woods, although it was not opened with any such intention," Donaldson wrote.

Applying the "first" label is risky. Orrin Fenton had a hotel at Number Four in Lewis County in 1826, a decade before Arnold's. Nothing tragic or exciting ever happened at Fenton's, according to Donaldson. It enjoyed a quiet popularity for many years and finally burned in 1965.

It was in 1826, too, that James Fenimore Cooper published *The Last of the Mohicans*, a work calculated to stimulate public curiosity about the Champlain country and the mountain wilderness that lay to the west. In 1837, Charles Fenno Hoffman wrote a glowing tribute to guide John Cheney, who, he said, ought to have been and perhaps was the model for Cooper's Natty Bumppo. On the other side of the mountains, A.L. Byron-Curtiss was to claim the same honor for Nat Foster. Cooper explained the genesis of Leatherstocking, his heroic man of the woods: "In a physical sense, different individuals known to the writer . . . certainly presented themselves as models . . . but in a moral sense this man of the forest is purely a creation." Later chroniclers of real-life stories of the great Adirondack guides probably owe more to the influence of Cooper and Leatherstocking than they might admit.

For an Adirondack guide, woodsman, or hotel keeper (who was often also a guide) to be famous, it was essential that competent, preferably professional, authors, poets, or journalists write about him and that the writings be published somewhere. The more writers a backwoodsman could attract, the more famous he might become, and thereby the more clients might seek his services or guests stay at his hotel. The guides were the heroes of the woods, noblemen of the forest, endowed with valor and worldly wisdom; their exploits, as recorded by admiring writers, were sometimes incredible. They were, along with the famous innkeepers, central figures in the Adirondack drama. For a "sport" to be on good terms with a great guide was as good as shooting a moose.

Jeptha R. Simms in *Trappers of New York* (1850) describes one such woodsman, Nick Stoner, as a man who "could kindle a fire, climb a tree, cook a dinner, empty a bottle, shoot a deer, hook a trout, or scent an Indian quicker than any white man then living." Alvah Dunning, who is supposed to have killed a hundred moose and 102 panthers, argued that the Earth must be flat, or the water in Raquette Lake, where he lived and worked as a hermit guide, would all spill out. Orson "Old Mountain" Phelps wasn't the most efficient guide in the region, but he was always good company. He liked to climb mountains to look at the view, and he didn't just go for "reg'lar walks" in the woods — he took "random scoots." The Moodys, Harvey, Mart, Will, Cort, and Phin, father and four sons, were a regular cartel. Mart imitated animal calls, and Will sometimes beguiled clients by singing a doleful ballad about the Massacre of Glencoe, which happened in Scotland in 1692. Harvey was chief guide for the redoubtable Lady Amelia Murray, maid of honor to Queen Victoria, whose exuberant progress from the Saranacs to Brown's Tract in 1855 stimulated other valiant women to yearn for similar adventure.

Charles Fenno Hoffman was probably the first to write about the Adirondacks for a wide audience, but Joel T. Headley's *The Adirondack; Or Life in the Woods* (1849) would stir a lethargic populace to action with rousing tales of wilderness derring-do. Headley, a pulpit preacher who became a New York City journalist and a fertile author of books, wrote vivid, readable descriptions of a glorious land of mountains, forests, and lakes. Edgar Allan Poe called him "the autocrat of all quacks," and Headley's busy pen seems, indeed, to have been dipped sometimes into Baron Munchausen's inkpot. Still, his *Adirondack* was popular and influential in its day. Reissued in 1982, it continues to attract critical attention. That Headley had a deep feeling for and love of nature there can be no doubt, but a skeptic must wonder at the unfailing good fortune which his hunters, fishermen, and guides always seemed to have. For example:

> My friend . . . did not fish over an hour and yet in that short time took
> a hundred and twenty pounds of trout and left them biting as sharp
> and fast as when he began . . . .. You can spend days and weeks

Alvah Dunning, by Seneca Ray Stoddard
Credit: The Adirondack Museum, Blue Mountain Lake, N.Y.

around the Raquette . . . taking trout at every cast . . . and killing a
deer whenever you choose to put forth the effort.

Headley's favorite guide, John Cheney, "one of the mildest, most unassuming
men you will meet with anywhere," nonetheless had some pretty breathtaking
adventures. The mild, unassuming Cheney, as Headley tells it, conquered a savage
she-wolf in hand-to-hand combat, while wearing snowshoes and with incidental
help from one of his two hounds. The other turned tail and ran. The wolf caused
Cheney to fall down during the battle, by stepping on his snowshoes. He defeated
an angry hibernating bear, again hand-to-hand and with the helpful dog pitching
in. Most harrowing, perhaps, was a face-to-face meeting with two charging
moose. "I heard a crashing through the bushes," Cheney told Headley, "and in a
minute more I saw both of them coming right towards me. As soon as they saw
me, they bent down their heads and made at me at full speed. The bushes and
saplings snapped under them like pipe stems. Just before they reached me, I
stepped behind a tree, and fired as they jumped by. The ball went through one and
lodged in the other."

These and other tales of instant pluck could be attributed to other guides, if the
guides, who were their own best publicists, could find willing ears to listen. But
not all guides were heroic or legendary; most worked without fanfare. Verplanck
Colvin hired more than fifty during his surveys in the 1870s, and a big hotel might
have had upwards of a hundred in residence or on call, with guide-boats and
hunting dogs to go with them.

All this — abundant fish and game easily taken, splendid scenery, colorful
narrators of tall stories, promises of adventure in the wilderness, physically
uncomfortable, perhaps, and slightly dangerous — was stimulating stuff for
world-weary city people. It was time to head for the woods, and to do that, the
eager pilgrims had to be assured of some kind of civilized hospitality before they
hit the trail. Tents, bark lean-tos, and run-down frontier dwellings wouldn't do.
There had to be real hotels — comfortable inns, or at least a respectable boarding
house.

Martin's was probably the first Adirondack hotel to be built expressly as a
popular summer resort. People said that Bill Martin was a fool to erect so big and
handsome a house in the wilderness, where only occasional hunters and
fishermen would see it. It was 1852, and the "Fashion" in those days was at
Saratoga Springs and Trenton Falls, where the "Quality" went to find
gratification, not on Lower Saranac Lake. But William F. Martin, who had been
renting Pliny Miller's unpretentious hotel since he came over from Malone a few
years before, thought he knew better.

Newspapers reported that Martin's hotel-raising was a grand, two-day affair.
Settlers came from thirty miles around, "many got gloriously drunk," and when it
was over, there stood a two-story frame structure, thirty-eight by thirty feet with a
twenty-four by thirty foot wing and accommodations for eighty. It was destined to
be one of the most popular and famous inns ever in the Adirondacks. A day was to
come when Martin's financial difficulties caused him to lose control of the hotel,
which continued to operate as Milo B. Miller's Saranac Lake House. Martin's, and

Miller's afterward, had grown to accommodate 250 guests, and was called "one of the far-flung gateways to the wilderness . . . . a most desirable tarrying place for all in quest of health or sporting recreation."

But one guest, a Boston newspaperman who called himself "Wachusett," found that the chief sport was to engage one of Martin's forty resident guides before someone else did, and to get away from the hotel, to chase deer in the forest, as quickly as possible. "The deer, with all their foolishness," he wrote, "have learned not to venture into the neighborhood of Lower Saranac Lake and venison is about as rare there as it is in Boston."

Hotels rose in rapid succession after Martin's. Before the end of the 1850s two of the most renowned, Bartlett's and the St. Regis Lake House, the latter known then and forever after as Paul Smith's, were open for business.

Vergil C. Bartlett was a man of rough exterior but with a twinkling eye and generous nature, once you got to know him. He succeeded Martin at Pliny Miller's, and then built his own place on the carry between Middle and Upper Saranac (Middle Saranac was called Round Lake then). Few woodland inns enjoyed as loyal a clientele as did Bartlett's. Many of Verge's guests, among them William A. Wheeler, vice president of the United States, returned year after year, for decades. A.B. Street, in *Woods and Waters; or the Saranac and Racket* (1860), wrote, on arriving at the carry,

> Here stood Bartlett's two story, unpainted frame tavern, and its shadow lay cool and black upon the gentle grassy slope . . . . Our guides were clustered at the open door of a log hut at one side, with several great hounds that, I found, belonged to Bartlett . . . , The boats and luggage having been carried over the portage to the Upper Lake, we followed, leaving Bartlett in the act of applying his right foot to the ribs of an unlucky hound, and the bulldog gazing after us with a face grim enough to darken daylight.

There was Baker's, a small inn on the Saranac River, with its "comfortable little parlor," where Amelia Murray rested, where Harvey Moody could tell how he "come 'crost the all-firedest big painter," while Mart did his animal calls and Will droned out a mournful lay about a Scottish massacre, after which everyone had tea around the chintz sofa of Baker's inner parlor, exchanging tales the while about deer they had shot and trout they had caught. Trout and venison, venison and trout — those were the watchwords in all the hotels.

In 1859, Apollos A. Smith, dynamic, enterprising son of a Vermont lumberman, built the St. Regis Lake House on Lower St. Regis Lake. It was the definitive Adirondack resort of the day, and Paul Smith the definitive guide and hotelier. No less a personage than Charles Dickens beat a drum for the formidable Paul by publishing in the September 29, 1860, issue of his magazine, *All the Year Round*, a laudatory article by an unnamed Adirondack traveler, which said in part:

He is a famous fellow, 'Pollos, or Paul, as he is called. Tall, athletic, and with no superfluous flesh about him, rawboned, with a good-natured twinkle in his blue eye, brimful of genuine Yankee humour, he had no bad habits, and is, withal, the best rifle shot, paddler, and compounder of forest stews in the whole region.

Paul Smith acquired ownership of more than thirty thousand acres of forest land with ten lakes and twenty-three miles of waterway. He was an accomplished story-teller; a few enthusiasts compared him to Mark Twain. He treated everyone alike, and had no awe of Very Important People. They flocked to his hotel, to be talked to, man-to-man, something a lot of them weren't used to. He had physical "presence" and a sure instinct for good public relations. Most important, perhaps, to the success of Paul Smith's venture was Lydia Martin Smith, Paul's wife, who was an excellent cook and who presided over a superb kitchen.

Paul Smith worked hard, and expected his employees to do so. He produced lumber from his own land and in his own sawmills, he built a power house to generate his own electricity, built his own electric railway to the nearest junction, ran his own stage line, got himself named postmaster of the "Paul Smiths" post office (traditionally spelled without an apostrophe), and kept the job through changing administrations. "There ain't no administration that can change faster than I can," Paul would proclaim. He was elected supervisor for the town of Brighton, Franklin County, and he became a millionaire.

Hotels and boarding houses continued to spring up in the woods as the Civil War came to an end, and a period of happy optimism set in. Then, in 1869, Rev. William H. H. Murray of Boston published *Adventures in the Wilderness; or, Camp Life in the Adirondacks* and went on the lecture circuit to extol the curative effects of breathing spruce-scented air and to praise Honest John Plumbley (or Plumley), his personal guide, and other stout-hearted woodsmen. Murray's book and his oratorical skills — said to rival those of Henry Ward Beecher — threw adventure-starved city folks into a dither and gave to Adirondack travel an entirely new impetus and to the author and instigator the permanent appellation "Adirondack Murray."

Boom times were at hand. Martin's, first point of contact for visitors arriving along the Hudson-Champlain-Keeseville route, met the "Murray Rush" head-on, and was almost swamped. Bill Martin had been fishing and was coming home with a good string of large trout when he saw the piazzas of his hotel filled to overflowing with people. He thought at first that there had been a funeral, or some other public event. A newspaper clipping in an old scrapbook recalls the day: "There were lots of nicely dressed ladies, and the men had on silk hats. He knew they were from the city." They were "Murray's visitors," vanguard of that army of outsiders who came to be known as "Murray's Fools." Sure enough, each of them was armed with a copy of Murray's new book and most had his complete regulation fishing outfit! It is recalled that the Delaware and Hudson Railroad made a practice of giving the Murray book to everyone who bought a D&H ticket to the Adirondacks.

As weeks passed, the Murray legions occupied every bed in every hotel, inn, and boarding house. They slept on porches, under trees, and among the shrubbery.

One story has it that a tired tourist paid the hourly rate for use of a billiard table as his bed. "Wachusett," the Boston newsman, wrote, "Mr. Murray's pen has brought a host of visitors into the wilderness such as it has never seen before; consumptives craving pure air, dyspeptics wandering after appetites, sportsmen hitherto content with small game and few fish . . . weary workers hungering for perfect rest . . . a multitude which crowds the hotels and clamors for guides and threatens to turn the wilderness into a Saratoga of fashionable costliness."

Saratoga had the Grand Union Hotel, with 1,500 beds and a ballroom with a $10,000 crystal chandelier; the United States Hotel had 1,200 beds and half a mile of piazza lined with rocking chairs. The ambience of Saratoga suggested a social one-upmanship which even Paul Smith's at its smartest might not match.

Frederick C. Durant may have had Saratoga in mind when he caused the Prospect House to be built at Blue Mountain Lake. This last word in lavish Adirondack hospitality opened for business on July 1, 1882. The Prospect House piazza was only 255 feet long, but it was the first hotel in the world to have Edison electric lights in all the bedrooms. Thomas Edison himself came to Blue Mountain Lake to supervise their installation. The hotel had steam heat and a steam-powered elevator, a two-story outhouse, and every luxurious accoutrement of a deluxe hostelry. "It was a remarkable and stupendous achievement," the historian Donaldson wrote. Wallace's *Guide*, after some hesitation, gave the Prospect House a rank even higher than Paul Smith's. "No structure of equal magnitude or magnificence has elsewhere been attempted," Wallace wrote. It was unusual also because it was thirty miles from a railway, and because it never burned down, not even during its lonely, ghostly abandonment, from 1903, when it quit receiving guests, until its demolition in 1915.

Wallace's 1887 *Guide* lists almost fifty hotels with more than one hundred beds. Joel Headley, on a return visit to the woods years after his first, found "long string of boats, fluttering with gay colors . . . Merry voices of maidens rang over the waters, rivalling the birds of the forest in sweetness of song. The effect of all this on the guides is amazing. The easy rollicking life these pleasure parties live, have [*sic*] made the guides lazy."

The guides might be "hotel guides," attached to and on the payroll of a single hotel. Large establishments, such as Paul Smith's, might have upwards of a hundred guides and guide-boats on hand. There were also "house guides," identified year after year with the same individual camp holders. Highest in the pecking order were the independent, sometimes very independent guides, who hired out to whomever they chose. The famous guides, Phelps, Dunning, Mitchell Sabattis, Plumley, Bill Nye, the Moodys, were usually independent. At the height of the social outburst after Murray, some hotel guides found themselves with demeaning, unprofessional assignments — rowing a grand lady with a parasol around a hotel pond, for instance. It goes without saying that some guides were more in demand than others.

For many among the thousands who went to the woods in those days, the hotels, in scenic surroundings, offering comfort, congenial company, relaxing entertainment, and good food, were resorts in the true sense, safe harbors for rejuvenation of mind, body, and spirit. For some, it is sad to say, they were bases

The Prospect House
Credit for both: The Adirondack Museum, Blue Mountain Lake, N.Y.

from which to wage merciless war against deer (jacklighting and hounding were common practice), trout, and other forest creatures. Some would calculate how to clear-cut virgin forests for profit; others wouldn't harm a squirrel or pick a red trillium in a swamp. For all, the inns were community centers; there a good idea might be born or an old prejudice die. There the seeds of future reform might take root.

From the beginning, small voices rose to protest against greed and rapacity. Samuel Hammond, an Albany journalist, wrote in 1857, "Had I my way . . . I would make (the region) a forest forever. It should be a misdemeanor to chop down a tree and a felony to clear an acre within its boundaries." *The New York Times* in an 1864 editorial proposed that the Adirondacks become a "Central Park for the World," but the proposal also suggested that within such a park, "the furnaces of our capitalists will line its valleys and create new fortunes to swell the aggregate of our wealth."

Verplanck Colvin, in his second survey report to the legislature, in 1847, wrote, "unless the region be preserved essentially in its present wilderness condition, the ruthless burning and destruction of the forests will slowly, year after year, creep onward after the lumberman, and vast areas of naked rock, arid sand and gravel will alone remain to receive the bounty of the clouds — unable to retain it." "Adirondack Murray" also had his say. "I could never bring my mind to pass a month in Maine . . . Go where you will in Maine, the lumbermen have been before you; and lumbermen are the curse and scourge of the wilderness."

The late Harvey L. Dunham, whose sympathetic understanding of the Adirondack mentality and temperament was unerring and whose *Adirondack French Louie* (1952) is one of the most satisfying of all books about home-grown Adirondackers, wrote,

> The Curtis Hounding Law, passed at Albany in the winter of 1884-85, was called by most hotel keepers the crowning act for the preservation of deer in the Adirondacks. Charles Fenton, hotel keeper of Number Four, said, 'I rejoice that this fall I shall not be compelled to report the bloody slaughter of deer by hounding.' But when fall came, the slaughter was worse than ever. Little attention was paid to the law, and hotel man Fenton was threatened with boycott by guides and hunters. Some hotel keepers even bought off game protectors so their guests could club hounded deer.

Dunham also wrote of a man who came out of the woods with fifty-seven pounds of trout, and that "not one of them was over seven inches . . . . Bushels of little trout taken from the headwaters of streams were shipped to New York, Boston, and Philadelphia markets."

Eventually, a strong guides' association was formed, with hundreds of members, "to aid and secure better enforcement of the game and forest laws of the state, to secure wise and practical legislation on all subjects affecting the game regions of the state; to secure the sportsman . . . competent and reliable guides, and to maintain a uniform rate of wages for guides." The organization, founded in

1898 as the Brown's Tract Guides Association, expanded its membership to cover all of the central Adirondacks.

Hotel life in the Adirondacks passed its zenith late in the nineteenth century. The times were changing. The very rich were breaking away to acquire acreage and build their own Great Camps. Others joined together to form clubs. The Adirondack League Club was formed in 1898 for "the preservation and conservation of the Adirondack region." It described itself as an "Adirondack Empire" of 275 square miles, eight times as large as Manhattan Island. Other "empires" of varying sizes were put together. Dr. W. Seward Webb's Mohawk and Malone Railroad penetrated the wilderness in the 1890s, and shortly after the turn of the century the first automobiles chugged into the Adirondacks, often on broken springs and with their share of flat tires.

Not all hotels, or even most of them, went out of business as times changed. But the flamboyant post-Murray period was done, leaving names to remember — Paul Smith, Verge Bartlett, Bill Martin, Ferd Chase of Loon Lake, Milo Miller, Smith Beede, Tyler Merwin and John Holland of Blue Mountain Lake, Otis Arnold, Gale, Roessle, Sturges, Kenwell, Wardner, Fenton, "Dut" Barber of Jock's Lake, and a host of others.

* *

As the doomed Forge House continued to burn on that July day sixty-one years ago, and as the battle to save it became futile, it is easy to imagine that one old-time Adirondacker might have said to another, as they watched the conflagration, "D'you s'pose this is the end of an era?"

Resources for the Taking

FLOY S. HYDE

In the beginning a varied and virgin growth covered the vast plateau that only in the nineteenth century would come to be known as the Adirondacks. Spruce, balsam, hemlock, pine, cedar, birch, maple, tamarack and aspen predominated. Alder, shadbush, cherry, basswood, willow, elm, butternut, sycamore, ash, ironwood, oak, chestnut and a score of other species, together with lower shrubs, added to the rich variety. In most places full-sized trees grew to the very tops of the mountains. Only a few peaks, among them Mount Marcy, showed a marked timber line with stunted growth above.

Today, of all the original wealth of forest, only a few small stands of virgin timber remain. The sizable trees one sees along the highways are, almost without exception, many decades removed from the original forests. Some of the second growth is so old as to seem itself like virgin timber; many places are now covered with third and fourth generations of replacement, the second having been lumbered many decades ago.

Early Lumbering

The earliest lumbering operations of commercial importance near the Adirondacks developed in the upper Hudson River valley, near Glens Falls, and along the Saranac River valley. Jacob Ferris built a little mill in 1787 at the mouth of the Saranac where it joined Lake Champlain. It was later sold to the Platt family, for whom Plattsburgh was named. Work moved farther up the upper Hudson and its tributaries after 1800, and Ticonderoga became the first great North Country town, although its wide reputation waned as the supply of profitable timber in the surrounding area was exhausted.

First to be consumed had been the tall, straight pines — sturdy, magnificent trees often growing to a height of two hundred feet and measuring seven feet at the base. England and France provided eager buyers for these giants of the forests and turned them into sturdy masts and beams for the fleets of ships they sailed around the world. Next to be sacrificed were spruces in all their handsome variety, primarily to meet the urgent demand in both foreign and domestic markets for high-quality sawed lumber.

As stands of commercially valuable timber in the Lake Champlain region decreased sharply, the push westward from the Hudson into the central Adirondacks intensified yearly. At the same time, incursions developed from other directions. Lumbering had begun on the lower Raquette River north of the Adirondacks about 1810. In the mid-1800s, the Maine Company of Boston built a large mill and established an extensive business at the northern end of Upper Saranac Lake, where Saranac Inn was ultimately located. But it was not until after 1850 that logging operations from all directions had reached the center of the Adirondacks, and it would not be very much longer before the last frontier of virgin forests — the northwest quadrant of the Adirondacks — would be exploited, with places such as Tupper Lake and Piercefield becoming new centers of the lumbering business.

From the outset, the state legislature contributed in varied and significant ways to the progress of these new industries. As early as 1806, the legislature declared

Tupper Lake, headquarters of the Adirondack lumber industry in the 1880s.
Credit: Harbor Hill Books, **History of the Lumber Industry in the State of New York**

the modest Salmon River in the Malone area a "public highway" open to lumbermen for transportation of their logs to sawmills downstream without regard to the complaints of irate property owners along the banks. Many other small rivers were so declared in the following years. In mid-century, the legislature appropriated funds for the building of many dams across small rivers, some not more than brooks, thus holding back both the natural flow and the big run-off of melting snows in the spring. With the opening of the dams, the heavy torrents provided swift transportation of logs to waiting mills. As an unfortunate consequence of the erection of these state dams, wide areas of timberland were flooded to several feet in depth. Trees were left standing, ultimately to die and become bare and gruesome ghosts rising from the stagnant waters. Later they were cut off at the waterline, but the hidden stumps remained a constant threat to public and private boats alike.

In still another instance, the state passed a law, in 1848, that entitled the Saratoga and Sacketts Harbor Railroad Company to purchase up to 250,000 acres of state land in Hamilton and Herkimer counties and to sell the timber thereon. The resulting capital was then to be used to develop a railroad line for the hauling of more timber to the waiting market. This pattern was followed by other and similar laws that encouraged business enterprises to profit substantially at the expense of public lands and forests.

Yet with all of this assistance, a major problem persisted — how to transport the raw materials of the Adirondacks to the mills effectively and economically. One of the earliest methods of moving logs was a true Adirondack "first." Log driving was originally practiced on the Schroon River branch of the upper Hudson in 1813. Fast-flowing streams, often with dangerous rapids, provided swiftly descending avenues for reaching desired destinations. The all-important cog in the process was the "logdriver." His task was one of great hardship and danger, with constant exposure to wind, weather, and ice-cold water. Logs could not be allowed to "jam up" on the shoreline or projecting rocks. If even one or two logs became lodged, hundreds of others piled up immediately. To break the impasse was the job of the logdriver who, with spiked, or calked, boots and an iron and wood tool called a peavy, leaped from one rolling, slippery log to another. Some lost their lives. French Canadians were said to be especially good at this work, and they were held in high regard by the industry.

Following the Civil War, an increasingly important aspect of the logging business became the harvesting of pulpwood for the making of paper. The wood first used was aspen, also called poplar and most often "popple" locally. But supplies were limited, and it was soon found that other species, spruce above all, were far better. The report of the State Forest Commission for 1879 shows 230,640,222 board feet of spruce alone used largely in the paper mills of the region. By 1914, New York State led the nation in pulp production, but a very sharp decline ensued, due largely to the growing scarcity of available timber.

Logging was big business, and its contribution to the wealth and growth of the state and nation is indisputable. As early as 1841, fifty-four lumber or "trade" yards were in operation in eleven Adirondack counties, supported by 1,459 sawmills and 7,000 to 8,000 lumberjacks, as workmen in the scores of lumber camps throughout the region were called. John Hurd built his "Big Mill" near Tupper Lake in the late 1800s. Said to be the largest sawmill ever built in New York State, it was a two-story structure, two hundred feet wide and four hundred feet long, with a capacity of 300,000 feet of lumber per day.

Unfortunately, heavy investment by management and the arduous labor of thousands of workers led not only to considerable commercial prosperity but also to dreary expanses of denuded mountainsides covered only with barren, broken trees and endless dry brush debris. Everything awaited the forest fire, which usually was not long in coming. Perhaps it is not surprising that the lumbermen were not greatly dismayed at the devastation, as the timber supply must have seemed literally without end, requiring only that operations at a depleted area pick up and move over the ridge to the next waiting mountainside of priceless timber.

Early Mining

In the field of mining, the Adirondack region can boast several impressive statistics. It had the largest open pit magnetite (iron ore) mine in the world at one time, the largest garnet mines in the world (at least until recently), the largest open pit ilmenite (titanium ore) mines in the world, the only commercial operation for the mining of wollastonite in the United States, the largest producers of commercial talc in the United States, and all of the zinc mined in New York State.

Of all the great variety of mineral deposits laid down eons ago in the Adirondacks, iron was always of primary importance, and it was iron production that was to have prodigious costs for Adirondack timberlands. Smelting required high heat, and charcoal produced from hardwoods such as maple, birch, and beech was the only practical way, in the early days, to achieve that high heat. Charcoal was produced in kilns, often known as "bee hives," located in the forests as near as possible to company forges. The kilns were made of brick and had an opening at the top. Four-foot wood was fed through this opening and arranged in criss-cross fashion. This was set on fire, the opening was covered, and the wood was kept smouldering for hours. At the proper time, water was poured onto the wood, and charcoal resulted. Each kiln burned an estimated one thousand cords of wood annually. The amount of wood consumed by all the mining operations in the Adirondacks over the years eludes estimation, however, because in addition to the vast operations conducted by large companies there were scores of small developments throughout the mountains. Each of these had its own little forge wherever a falls offered water power and a sawmill was close at hand to cut up timber for charcoal. It was fortunate for what remained of the timberlands that coke, a much cheaper material than charcoal, came into general use nationally about 1903.

The product that resulted from the use of charcoal for smelting was known as "charcoal pig iron," and it was widely recognized for its superiority. At the 1893 Chicago World's Fair, the Chateaugay Ore and Iron Company won the highest award for the quality of its magnetite concentrates.

Of the iron mines that developed in the Adirondacks, the Cheever Mine, north of Port Henry on Lake Champlain, was reportedly the first commercial development, beginning around 1750. Benedict Arnold is said to have ordered ore from the Cheever Mine to be made into iron for outfitting vessels that later were engaged in the first naval battles in the War for Independence. The Arnold Hill mines, near Ausable Forks, were in operation as early as 1806 and the nearby Palmer Hill mines in 1825. By 1842, the extensive works of the Peru Iron Company, located in the village of Clintonville, boasted a forge of eighteen fires, an extensive rolling mill, a nail factory, and a cable factory.

Another large iron mining operation with a quite different fate came into being in the east-central Adirondacks near Lake Sanford in the town of Newcomb, about 1830. It was founded by Archibald McIntyre and his associate, Judge Duncan McMartin, and it became known as the Adirondac Iron Works. Many difficulties beset the enterprise. From beginning to end, the excessive cost of transportation to markets was a major handicap, despite the building of a road through thirty miles of unbroken forest to Crown Point on Lake Champlain. Another difficulty was presented by an unidentified "impurity" in the ore, and this, along with a flood and the financial panic of 1857, proved decisive in the closing of the mine. The "impurity" was identified as titanium, but it would be another eighty-four years before the mine was reopened, largely because of World War II, so that this important whitening agent could play its part in the production of paint, tires, paper, and other products.

Another of the Lake Champlain mining developments was the Crown Point Company, first formed in 1844. It came to own outright the villages of Hammondville and Ironville as well as the settlements associated with its charcoal kilns, Chilson Hill, Blackman Settlement, and Black Brook. General John Hammond was the moving force in the corporation. He ultimately consolidated his operations with those of other mine owners in the area, until together they formed an iron mining and manufacturing company best described as a "colossus" for those early times. The first steel made in this country under the Bessemer patents is said to have been made from this company's product.

Despite its one-time prosperity, The Crown Point Iron Company declined and finally went out of business in the late nineteenth century. The panics of 1873, 1883 and 1893, the opening of mines in the Mesabi Iron Range in Minnesota, severe labor troubles, and a variety of business difficulties led at last to its demise. The Chateaugay Ore and Iron Company and the Delaware and Hudson Canal Company took it over for a while, but the mine closed permanently in 1896. The seemingly endless deposit of ore was practically exhausted, and the prospects for a new supply were almost nonexistent.

Prominent in the total development of iron mining was an operation at Lyon Mountain, on the northern edge of the Adirondacks. The ore bed had been discovered about 1823, but it was not developed until it was bought by the Chateaugay Ore Company in 1872. Only eleven years later, twenty fires were in operation at a location called merely "The Forge." This operation constituted the largest Catalan forge in the world. "Catalan" signified an open hearth fired by charcoal for the smelting of the iron, which would ultimately be poured into blooms or billets. These were pieces of iron about five inches square and from two to six feet long, ready for shipment. The company also supplied numerous other forges in Franklin, Clinton, and Essex counties, making a total of sixty fires burning at one time.

To provide an adequate supply of charcoal, the management acquired 150,000 acres of timberland, largely through tax sales held by the state. It is estimated that, from the founding of the mine until coke came to be utilized for the fires, some 1,500,000 solid cords, or roughly 135,000,000 cubic feet of wood, were used in the production of charcoal. In addition, fifteen thousand cords of four-foot spruce and balsam pulp were sold to paper mills annually.

Iron ore from the mines at Lyon Mountain was loaded into wagons and hauled over a plank road to a dock on Upper Chateaugay Lake. It was then transferred to a big barge called *Iron Age*, which was eighty feet long and seventeen feet wide and carried 150 tons of ore. *Iron Age* was towed by a little steamer named *Maggie* to The Forge at the outlet of Lower Chateaugay Lake. Arriving at its destination, the ore had to be transferred by hand to a small car that was drawn by a cable to the stockpiles at the various small forges making up the total operation. Each fall before the close of navigation, enough ore was stored to run the forges during the winter. Ten fires were kept in year-round operation.

The Forge, with a population of some eight hundred persons, prospered mightily. It had a post office, store, hotel, school, and about fifty houses. Other dwellings were strung out along the main road for at least a mile. Not everything was crude in origin; the Moffit House was a colonial mansion, complete with marble fireplaces and plastered cornices. Operations at The Forge required many horses and the fodder to feed them. Blacksmith, wheelwright, and sled shops were busy. Sawmills hummed and whined continuously. Boat shops flourished, turning out tug boats and passenger boats, many powered by steam, as well as large numbers of rowboats, some still in use. Several miles of road, constructed of three-inch planking, were built northward to Chateaugay; a telegraph line was put through.

Blooms and billets of iron were hauled by wagons and sleighs to Chateaugay and shipped to the steel districts of Pennsylvania and Ohio. Records from the 1880s indicate a large number of Chateaugay blooms being shipped to the manufacturers of the wire for the Brooklyn Bridge. Much later, fifteen thousand tons of Chateaugay iron were used to manufacture the steel cable for the George Washington Bridge at New York City.

The village of Lyon Mountain, at the site of the mines, grew from a few log shacks in the wilderness to a thriving community of some three thousand persons. Increased production made proportionate demands for charcoal, and it was ncessary to reach still farther into the forests for timber adequate to meet the growing need. In 1885, the company began the erection of a blast furnace at Standish. The pig iron produced from this furnace was a quite different product from the bloom iron produced by the Catalan forge. Prosperity increased in Standish, and many new houses, a store, a school house, and a church sprang up in the little village. On many a summer evening the sky was aflame with the glow of the blast furnace at Standish as it poured out the white hot metal, often as much as sixty tons, into the great container waiting to receive it.

A decline in all of this prosperity became inevitable ultimately. The cost of transporting the product to markets, expensive deep-shaft mining to a depth of sixteen hundred feet, and competition from both western mines and foreign imports all contributed to a gradual slowing of operations. Finally, in June, 1966, nearly a hundred years after its opening, the mine was permanently closed. At The Forge, a small marker, almost hidden by surrounding brush, reads, "On this site was built in 1874 the world's largest Catalan forge, abandoned in 1893." Only a handful of people can remember it was ever there.

Early Railroading

It was not until after the Civil War that railroads penetrated the Adirondacks. In 1868, a line from Plattsburgh reached Point of Rocks; by 1874 it had been extended to Ausable Forks. The Adirondack Railroad reached North Creek from Saratoga in 1871, and by 1875 construction of the Delaware & Hudson mainline had been completed along the western shore of Lake Champlain — the eastern edge of the Adirondacks. Tracks were laid from Plattsburgh to Dannemora in 1879; the owners of the mines at Lyon Mountain built a connecting link, and the combined route became known as the Chateaugay Railroad. In following years, it was extended through Standish and Loon Lake to Saranac Lake. Charcoal from kilns along the route was hauled to forges, ore was transported, billets of iron were shipped, and lumber camps prospered as the line provided easy transportation to markets.

Another early railroad, known as the Northern Adirondack, or as "Hurd's Road" after its builder, John Hurd, was laid entirely within Franklin County. It was begun in 1883 and developed in small sections until it ran from Moira to Tupper Lake. Its chief purpose was to haul vast quantities of logs from the lumber camps to Hurd's huge mill at Tupper Lake.

Inasmuch as the locomotives were dependent on wood and later on coal, one result was inevitable — frequent bursts of sparks and live coals from stack and fire-box flew deep into live forests and denuded lands alike. While other factors such as lightning and man's carelessness shared some of the responsibility, railroads in the early days were regarded as the chief cause of Adirondack fires. Many extensive timber tracts were swept by fire during the last quarter of the nineteenth century.

A fire once started in a partially lumbered area can seldom be contained. It tears through adjacent woodlands and often into farm areas, where crops and buildings add to the holocaust. A forest fire is one of nature's most awesome sights, as the blaze roars its way through the magnificent evergreens, which flame to the sky like so many colossal torches. All creatures flee in terror before it or succumb helplessly.

In the old days, owners of camps and summer hotels were constantly on the alert, as their properties were often threatened. Sometimes it was necessary to vacate on short notice. One veteran of the Adirondacks said, "I well remember a big forest fire. It followed the railroad tracks for a long distance. People crawled down the tracks for seven miles, wrapped up in cloths or anything else that would provide a bit of protection for their hands and knees. When close to the ground, they could manage to breathe but couldn't stand up because of the smoke."

Passenger traffic on the main lines was heavy for many years, but more important was the hauling of vast quantities of logs, lumber, pulp, ore, iron, and all kinds of merchandise and supplies by the many freight trains that plied the tracks every day. The arrival of a passenger train, especially a "through" train during the summer season, was akin to the arrival of the stagecoach in some parts of the country in earlier days. Long whistles of the approaching engines whetted the excitement, and the clatter of arrival filled the air. Passengers piled off and piled on, all with appropriate hullabaloo. A rackety express wagon transferred its varied cargo of suitcases and queer-looking boxes aboard. Mail bags were exchanged, with quick pleasantries going both ways. At last, with proper fanfare, the noisy monster of a train took off.

With the advent of the railroads, tiny hamlets often grew into sizable settlements. Conifer, west of Tupper Lake, was an example of an almost symbiotic relationship between lumbering and railroading. Established in 1882 by the Emporium Lumber Company, Conifer became a thriving village, widely known for its vast lumbering operations. There were dwelling houses for fifty families, a boarding house, store, large hotel, post office, railroad station, school, church, doctor's office, pool hall, and soda fountain.

Beyond all doubt, it was the railroads that opened up the Adirondacks — to tourism and travel, fishing and hunting, business and trade, and all the opportunities for personal growth, sometimes including recovery of health — for all those who wished so much to come into the Adirondacks before the days of the automobile. As with lumbering and mining, railroading was both big business and a way of life, but it also took its own distinctive toll of the woodlands and of the great wilderness.

Almost as soon as heavy logging and intensive railroading had penetrated deep into the Adirondacks, and mining had begun to take its toll, voices came to be raised in protest and alarm. Shippers in Albany, at the time the largest lumber port in the world, were justifiably fearful of running out of prized Adirondack timber. In New York City, civic organizations were considering the danger to the general water supply and to the Hudson River in particular. Sportsmen and innkeepers in the Adirondack region itself were becoming worried about the rapidly vanishing beauty and challenges of the wilderness. Still, it was to be twenty years before protective action was finally taken.

Before the 1860s, few had been the advocates of protection. Later, with far more cause for alarm, it is surprising how long it was before concrete steps were taken. Progress toward passage of the Forest Preserve law was made against great odds. As one small example, lumber interests had been eagerly buying state lands for very small sums, removing the timber, and then allowing them to revert to the state for unpaid taxes; passage of a "forever wild" measure would spell the end of such practices. Despite protests and in response to the vigorous support of its advocates, the measure did become law. Henceforth, state-owned lands, which would eventually constitute nearly forty percent of the Adirondack area, would be forever safe from inroads, to remain a heritage beyond price for all the foreseeable future.

Fathers of the Forest Preserve

NEAL S. BURDICK

As the winter of 1864-65 succumbed to spring, there was optimism in the land. The Civil War was winding down, prosperity abounded — at least in the North — and people turned their sights once again ahead, determined to pick up the pace of Manifest Destiny. A vast continent, ripe with resources, awaited — and conservation was a word not yet imagined.

Just twenty years later, conservation commanded significant attention, if not universal acceptance, and hundreds of thousands of forested acres in the Adirondacks, as well as the Catskills, had been by law declared "forever wild," off limits to the lumber barons of the times. How did this radical transformation come about in so short a time that lands that were in the 1860s popularly assumed to be there for the plucking were a mere two decades later themselves plucked from the hands of those who would exploit them?

No such revolution in thinking happens overnight, nor is it so simple that individuals can be assigned credit for it. But the fact remains that several trends in the first two-thirds of the 1800s produced the atmosphere in which such a change could take place. And it can be argued that, among all those who played a part in the channeling of this new attitude into the creation of the Adirondack Forest Preserve, four men stand out: George Perkins Marsh, Verplanck Colvin, Franklin B. Hough, and Charles Sprague Sargent.

First, the trends. Keep in mind that anything remotely like a positive attitude toward wilderness — that is, one that says it is not necessary to destroy the wilderness in the name of progress — is a very recent phenomenon in human history. As historians such as Roderick Nash have pointed out, for most of man's existence, wilderness — whether it be the forests of the north or the deserts of the Middle East or the oceans in between — was both physically and spiritually inhospitable, threatening, barren, devoid of light, home to evil spirits, and so on. Wilderness was all things that civilization was not. Therefore it was an obstacle, a thing to be removed. This point of view was brought to the New World by the Puritans, who applied it with a vengeance, in part because they expected to find a new Garden of Eden and not the "howling wilderness," as one of their early theocrats called it, that they did find.

The Puritan legacy survived well into the nineteenth century, and indeed it survives still, but during the nineteenth century it began to be tempered by numerous forces. First and foremost, by the nineteenth century Americans had developed their social and economic fabric to the point that wilderness was no longer a barrier to success. The gains of the Agricultural Revolution and the Industrial Revolution took care of that. Wilderness ceased also to be a physical threat, at least in those places where most of the population resided. A pioneer on the leading edge of the frontier might not agree, but to an affluent family enjoying life in its home on Fifth Avenue or Beacon Hill, wilderness was the last thing they need fear.

James Fenimore Cooper was one of the first to express this notion, when in his plodding way in the Leatherstocking Tales he questioned whether it were necessary to cut down every tree in sight, and whether his mythical wilderness personification Natty Bumppo — who saw action in the southeastern Adirondacks in *The Last of the Mohicans* — could not find a place in society. That idea was too much for the conservative Cooper, and he banished Bumppo to the West — but not without some regret.

Cooper had helped sow a seed that would take root and flower in later years in the writings of men such as Emerson, Thoreau and Bryant, who suggested that wilderness has values that render it worthy of being left alone, if not actively preserved. Others came to feel that it could be preserved, without harm to society. In the Adirondacks, these people included, among others, those who wanted the wilderness left as it was so they could hunt, fish, relax and contemplate, and those who learned they could find relief from respiratory diseases in the pure air of the forest — as well as those who discovered they could make a living off of the desires of those people. The hotels that sprouted on the shores of many an Adirondack lake, and the health resorts, most notably Dr. Edward Livingston Trudeau's famous Adirondack Cottage Sanitorium, which came into being almost simultaneously with the Forest Preserve, are testimony to the presence of these people.

But the wish to spend part of the summer "in camp," and even the desire to go to the mountains "to take the cure," were not enough to move politicians, who heard also — and more clearly at first — from the lumbermen, the mining entrepreneurs, and the speculators. These people were indignant that a perfectly good, centuries-old tradition, one that allowed them unquestioned access to the riches of the wilderness, should suddenly be challenged by a collection of preachers, one-legged journalists and half-dead invalids. A more compelling reason to preserve the wilderness was needed. Full appreciation of wilderness had to grow from concerns of the pocketbook as well as the mind and the soul.

Marsh

The rather unlikely individual who provided the economic incentive for environmental protection in general was a near-sighted, bookish Vermonter named George Perkins Marsh. A mediocre lawyer and a failure as a businessman, he found his niche as a congressman and diplomat, and fame as the author in 1864 of *Man and Nature, or Physical Geography as Modified by Human Action*, which historian Lewis Mumford later called "the fountainhead of the conservation movement." In this long, ponderous book Marsh introduced to the American people the concept of ecology and the notion of resource conservation, thereby changing the way they looked at the world around them.

The year before Marsh was born, in 1801 in Woodstock, Vermont, forest fires destroyed most of the timber in that area. A new forest and he grew up together, and Marsh had a continuing lesson in natural reforestation. When the forest matured it was logged, and Marsh observed that the removal of the tree cover from the steep slopes resulted in the rapid runoff of rainwater, and especially melting snow, which in turn caused floods that ruined the agricultural economy in the valleys below. Later, during twenty-one years as Minister to Italy, Marsh noted that the Italians had learned their lesson: mountain slopes had been reforested; through selective harvesting a supply of timber was guaranteed in perpetuity, and the flow of water off the slopes was much more moderate, steady and useful. It was a lesson he hoped to convey to Americans before it was too late.

Marsh was at heart a utilitarian, not a romantic: wilderness *per se* had little value as far as he was concerned. Others who considered themselves utilitarians in the mid-1800s thought conservation an extravagance: lumber kings, for example, found it much more expedient to "strip and run" than to cut selectively. But Marsh argued for conservation precisely on utilitarian terms. The forests, he explained, would be even more commercially productive with less harvesting, because they would be healthier. It was managed forest, not wilderness, that he proposed.

From Burlington, where he had his law office, Marsh could see the skyline of the Adirondacks across Lake Champlain to the west. Thus it is not surprising that the Adirondacks figured in his scheme of revolutionizing the way Americans treated resources. In fact, the Adirondacks were to his mind the perfect laboratory in which his ideas might be applied. Discussing the possibility of protecting the forests of the Adirondacks, he wrote, "Nature threw up these mountains and clothed them with lofty woods, that they might serve as a reservoir to supply with perennial waters the thousand rivers and rills that are fed by rains and snows of the [highlands]." Forests on mountain slopes, he contended, assure a supply of water to the farms and cities in the drainage basins that extend from the mountains to the ocean   a point that was sure to catch the attention of the millions who depended upon the Adirondack watershed for drinking water, for farming, and for commerce on the Erie Canal and Hudson River.

Marsh proposed two ways to bring about such protection: sound forest management, including selective cutting and reforestation, by the harvesters; and, failing that, purchase for the purpose of management by the government. The latter was a radical idea in 1864, and one that still elicits vociferous opposition, but Marsh felt the government was the only agent powerful enough to contain the greed of individuals and corporations that lacked any incentive to check themselves.

Marsh was not wholly against wilderness preservation for its own sake. Speaking again of the Adirondacks, he wrote that "such a large and easily accessible region of American soil" should be protected not only for economic reasons but also for fulfilling such non-utilitarian purposes as

> A museum for the instruction of the student, a garden for the recreation of the lover of nature, and an asylum where indigenous tree, and humble plant that loves the shade, and fish and fowl and four-footed beast, may dwell and perpetuate their kind, in the imperfect protection as the laws of a people jealous of restraint can afford them.

In this manner he built a bridge that leaped the chasm between those who supported preservation for reasons primarily pragmatic and those who supported it for reasons generally more altruistic.

Among the many who were influenced to some degree by Marsh, perhaps no one was such a crusader for legislative protection of the Adirondacks than Verplanck Colvin. Born in 1847 into a distinguished and influential Albany family, Colvin studied law obediently but roamed the out-of-doors and learned forest ecology passionately. As a young man he traveled in many parts of the United States, sending accounts of his expeditions to *Harper's* magazine and Albany newspapers. He also explored the Adirondacks, and it was the Adirondacks that captured his true devotion. As early as 1868 he was agitating for protection of the region's forests. In 1870, in a report to the state Board of Regents on his ascent of Mt. Seward, which was the first recorded ascent and barometrical determination of the elevation of that peak, he argued, in language that reads much like Marsh's, that "the Adirondack wilderness contains the springs which are the sources of our principal rivers and the feeders of the canals," that the "destruction of the forests" would deprive the land "of all that gives it value," and that "the remedy for this is the creation of an Adirondack Park or timber reserve . . .. The interests of commerce and navigation," he concluded, "demand that these forests should be preserved; and for posterity should be set aside, this Adirondack region, as a park for New York, as is the Yosemite for California and the Pacific states."

Noting that commercial interests dependent upon the state's canals were complaining about the decreasing flow of water in the Mohawk-Hudson watershed, Colvin argued early and often that forest preservation was essential to their economic survival:

> The practical continuance of the canals or their enlargement for shipping purposes, . . . depends in the future, . . . on the numerous rivers of the wilderness; and there is not a builder, or a farmer throughout the state but is interested in preserving from . . . destruction the vast forest . . . of northern New York . . . .

From 1873 on he argued, like a school teacher drilling stubborn youngsters, that "the summit of the watershed of the Hudson" was "the area of forest which it is necessary to preserve in order to protect from evaporation the springs and streams which are the sources of the Hudson." Colvin hammered away at this theme until the Adirondack Forest Preserve became a reality in 1885, and even beyond; although many people played important parts in that drama, no one did more to sway public opinion through a public relations campaign that verged on the evangelistic than did he.

Like Marsh before him, Colvin was inclined toward the utilitarian side of the preservation argument. While he was capable of outright viciousness toward civilization in general, he also lauded such advancements in the mountains as "stage-coach (lines), . . . numerous railroads (and) magnificent hotels, metropolitan in character . . . ." Thus he hoped that any action taken would be

Verplanck Colvin
Credit: The Adirondack Museum, Blue Mountain Lake, N.Y.

. . . truly preservative of the forest, but not in any way interfering with the natural trade and commerce of the country. The true course would be to set aside for the purposes of the Adirondack park or State forest reservation, all the untillable, rocky and mountainous lands upon the sources of the Hudson, without touching one cleared farm or fertile valley.

Colvin felt strongly that such a preserve should not be a hindrance to resource recovery. "What harm if valuable beds of (iron or other) metals should be discovered and developed?" he asked. He also believed that private property should not be pre-empted by the state, unless the property lay on terrain absolutely critical to watershed protection, in which case it "should be made subordinate to the public interests." Colvin thus advocated a concept in which individuals were allowed to live and carry on commerce within the boundaries of the preserve. The Adirondack State Park, established in 1892, was the first administrative unit where this idea was put into practice, and the federal government adopted it, over the objections of strict preservationists, when it established national forest reserves (called simply national forests today) in the 1890s.

Colvin had first visited the Adirondacks in 1865. By predilection an explorer of untrammeled places, he was dismayed at the poor quality of existing maps of the region. He determined to correct this deficiency, and began an informal survey of the Adirondacks. By 1872 he had decided to perform a complete topographical survey of the Adirondacks, and had used his persuasiveness and his connections in Albany to extract funding from the legislature. He continued his survey for twenty-eight stormy years, during which time it was expanded to include an accurate marking of the boundaries of state-owned land in the region — a necessary prelude to the delineation of a forest preserve. At the end of each year Colvin submitted to the legislature a detailed report of his progress. Although for the most part these reports were predictably ignored, through the sheer force of the data they contained and the language in which they were written they ultimately had much influence in the creation of the Forest Preserve. Colvin knew the power of the pen, and he could fashion an evocative image when he sensed it could sway a wavering politician. When he discovered the highest source of the Hudson River in 1872, he described it as "a minute, unpretending tear of the clouds"; only the most hard-nosed pragmatist could have turned his back on the principle of preserving the forests around such a spot. Eventually, Lake Tear-of-the-Clouds became the official name of this tiny pond high on the southwest slope of Mt. Marcy.

Colvin's goals in conducting the Adirondack Survey were essentially those that Marsh had outlined when he advocated scientific study of forest ecosystems. "This survey," Colvin wrote in 1886, the year after the creation of the Forest Preserve, "is . . . intended . . . to furnish data for the state government for the better management of public lands." He believed that the rapid development of such a large region made it incumbent upon the state to provide guidance over that development, in the interest of all concerned.

Colvin advocated a revolutionary change of course in America's attitude toward forest use. In his report for 1874, he articulated how this attitude should do an about-face: taking his cue from Marsh, he urged

> that a trial be made (of reforestation), for I feel sure that in ten years the people would be astonished at the result. Enterprise is an American characteristic and in our early days was characterized by tree destruction; now, in the preservation of forests we must learn from Europe that economy which experience has dictated.

In order to assure that this step take place, Colvin again sided with Marsh in calling for (and soon defending) the equally revolutionary procedure of ownership of forest lands by the state government. As lumber companies abandoned their cut-over holdings, he said, the state should assume possession and then retain the parcels, instead of selling them as it was then customary to do.

While Colvin was first and foremost a utilitarian, he departed from many of his associates who were, perhaps unwittingly, creating the new field of forestry, when he backed preservation on aesthetic and spiritual as well as practical grounds. He was a man who loved life in intimate contact with nature, the more wild the better. Like Thoreau, he luxuriated in vistas from mountain summits where "no clearings were discernible, wilderness everywhere . . ." To Colvin the wilderness was a place of solitude and mystery, yet it could speak to man, telling him of the roots of life, the sources of knowledge:

> . . . we gaze down from the mountain height on . . . thousands of square miles of wilderness, which was always one — since forest it became — and which hides today, as it has hidden for so many ages, the secrets of form, . . . and history, on which we ponder.

Although he had a mission, that mission was to varying degrees a means to an end for Colvin. It was a convenient reason to avoid the world of business, politics and fashion — in which he was not comfortable — and spend his time in the company of a few trusted colleagues and down-to-earth guides roaming the wild woods and peaks of the Adirondacks. At times his reports read like adventure tales, replete with surprise encounters with snarling panthers, terrifying night descents down icy rock faces, and swirling forest fires (which he himself had set, as a means of clearing summits for use as surveying stations). Like the romantic writers and artists of a generation earlier, Colvin found in the wilderness the epitome of the inspirational setting:

> Before us an irregular cone of granite, capped with ice and snow, arose against a wintry sky . . . . On either side the icy slopes leaped at once down into gloomy valleys. Beyond, irregularly grouped, the great peaks grizzly with frost and snow — were gathered in grand magnificence, all strange and new — in wild sublimity. No sound save the shuddering hiss of the chilly blast as it swept over the

fearful ridge of ice that now must be our pathway.

The force of these impressions was so great that by late in his career Colvin was arguing for the preservation of some areas of great scenic beauty and of pristine wilderness as well as of critical watersheds. Thus, while he continued to champion the preservation of resource-yielding forest lands through sound management practices, he also came to accept the spiritual and aesthetic dimensions of the wilderness as worthy of salvation also. Colvin's ability to blend these elements marks him as a catalyst in the growing acceptability of a positive attitude toward wilderness in the final decades of the nineteenth century. His multiple vision is best seen in this description of the area that he considered most deserving of preserve status:

> It forms but a small portion of this northern forest region; is acknowledged to be cold, sterile, and useless for farming; it embraces the sources of the Hudson River and lakes already used as reservoirs by lumbermen; and besides contains the highest mountains of New York — a region of wonderful beauty and picturesqueness which, under control as a park, and preserved from ruthless destruction by fire, can be made . . . profitable to this State by travel and traffic . . . .

Colvin enjoyed considerable support from a variety of quarters. Influential publications as diverse as *The American Sportsman, Forest and Stream*, and *Engineering and Mining Journal* gave extensive coverage to his work and editorialized in favor of his preservation plans. Newspapers in the Adirondacks did likewise: Colvin was lauded as "the hero of the North Woods," credited with superhuman feats of exploration and discovery, and praised for untangling the maze of indefinite boundaries between state and private lands. The local press urged support of his calls for tougher game laws and preservation of the forests, although for economic rather than ecological or cerebral reasons. Similar concerns elicited continuing support from such business organizations as the New York Board of Trade and Transporation, which brought its weight to bear on the legislature throughout Colvin's fight to give legal protection to the Adirondack watersheds. Further dissemination of Colvin's ideas came in the form of the numerous guidebooks for vacationers in the Adirondacks that became best-sellers among the large numbers of well-to-do people who turned the Adirondacks into the nation's most desirable resort in the 1870s and 1880s.

On the other hand, Colvin drew widespread criticism from interests that felt threatened by his scheme of preservation. Much resentment came from residents of the Adirondacks, who were opposed, for economic reasons as well as in principle, to anything suggesting regulation of the forests and their free access to them. They had no sympathy with the Marsh-Colvin doctrine that the government was the best manager of forest lands.

Except for Governor John A. Dix, who urged the legislature to act upon Colvin's recommendations in 1874, the state's executive branch was oblivious at best and hostile at worst toward his ideas. However, largely at Colvin's instigation an array of environmentally beneficial legislation was enacted in the 1880s and 1890s aside from the Forest Preserve law itself. One law provided tax compensation for local governments in areas where the state took over possession of land, the effect of which was — and is — to deflate the objection that land acquisition by the state hurts local tax revenues. Another, which today might be called clean water legislation, in the quaint language of the times placed strict controls on the discharge of "dye-stuff, coal tar, refuse from gashouses, saw dust, lime or other deleterious substance" into the state's rivers.

But it was in the achievement of the Forest Preserve that Colvin had his greatest success with the legislature, although the end result was not what he had envisioned. The first legal victory for preservation came in 1883, when a bill to halt the sale of state land, with an appropriation to begin repossessing land, was passed. An elated Colvin reacted that the law was "directly in accordance with the recommendations made by the Commission of State Parks in their report of May 14, 1873 . . . ," which he had had a hand in writing. This was followed two years later by the monumental Forest Preserve Act of 1885, which Adirondack historian William Chapman White later called "the foundation of American forestry."

Colvin's was essentially a late-nineteenth-century mind, concerned with science, business and productive management of forests. Yet he also expounded views that are normally associated with twentieth-century thinkers — primarily, that wilderness has values above and beyond the purely practical. Thus he was one of the first to give significant weight to many of the arguments used by both professional conservationists and ecologists and amateur environmental activists today: protection of timber supplies, control of erosion, recreation, aesthetic appreciation, spiritual health. It is symbolic of his overall perspective that he felt the most useful result of his work was the publication of small, highly detailed topographic maps that could be used by engineers, foresters, sportsmen and Sunday afternoon hikers alike.

Hough

One associate of Colvin's who had a mutually influential relationship with him was Dr. Franklin B. Hough. It may have been he who impressed upon Colvin the importance of Marsh's thinking, although Colvin may already have arrived at some of the same conclusions through his own observation and through his reading of others' works.

Hough was, like many of the actors in the drama of the birth of the Forest Preserve, a man of eclectic interests and abilities and limitless energy. A doctor in Lowville, in the Black River valley on the western edge of the Adirondacks, he was also a student of natural history, meteorology, botany and mineralogy, the author of voluminous histories of four northern New York counties (Franklin, St. Lawrence, Jefferson and his own Lewis) and of a massive 1873 gazetteer of New York State, supervisor of the state census in 1855 and 1865, and originator and first head of what is now the United States Forest Service.

As for the Adirondacks, Hough was a member of the 1872 Commission of State

Parks, created by the legislature "to inquire into the expediency of providing for vesting in the State the title to the timbered regions lying within (seven Adirondack counties) and converting the same into a public park." This was the commission of which Colvin was secretary; it is likely that Hough had much to say when it came time in 1873 to write the commission's report, whose language and tone of urgency were likely Colvin's but whose emphasis on forest management, not wilderness preservation, was strongly promoted by Hough. The commissioners sought forest protection on George Perkins Marsh's terms — for the perpetuation of a water supply for farms and for the Erie Canal, and for the prevention of devastating spring floods. They granted that recreation in such a managed forest was perfectly acceptable, but stated in no uncertain terms that a park such as Yellowstone, which President Ulysses S. Grant had signed into being the year before, would be "unproductive and useless." An Adirondack park, they argued, should be open to resource harvesting. This was how Hough envisioned a properly managed forest.

Twelve years later, with the Forest Preserve about to become a reality, Hough further elucidated his position. In discussing the opposition to the Forest Preserve proposal, he said:

> This opposition, I believe, would be changed to firm support if the true end and aim of forestry were rightly understood. It is *not* the object of forestry, at least in this country, to maintain the woodlands as a shelter for game and as a region of pleasure resort to those who can afford the time and means for this kind of enjoyment . . . . Our taxpayers would never tolerate such an object of expense, and it is to be regretted that the word "park" has ever been used in this connection, because it leads to the erroneous idea that expenses are to be increased for the enjoyment of those who have time or money to spend in sporting or in woodland life.
>
> We regard the principal and by far the most important end of forestry to be the growth of timber for the supply of man.

Hough's point of view in fact carried the day when it came time for the legislature to vote the Forest Preserve into being.

Sargent

The report that was issued by the Commission of State Parks in 1873 was, as so often happens to such documents, consigned to an obscure shelf where it gathered dust. But it provided the groundwork for a future body, one whose work did result in the creation of the Forest Preserve. This was known as the Sargent Committee, after its chairman and most active participant, Charles Sprague Sargent. Sargent was a pioneer dendrologist, prime mover behind Harvard University's famed Arnold Arboretum, and author of the fourteen-volume *Silva of North America*, a project it took him twenty years to complete. Before he became involved with the Adirondacks he garnered some experience by orchestrating a study of the nation's forest resources for inclusion in the 1880 federal census.

106

Sargent's work in the creation of the Adirondack Forest Preserve has been too little noted. Although it has not yet been so proven, many historians think it may have been Sargent who conceived the famous "forever wild" language that characterized the 1885 Forest Preserve law and that was entered into the constitution of New York State in 1894.

The so-called Sargent Committee was appointed primarily because continuing abuses of the Adirondack forests, and continuing concern about the downstate water supply, kept before the public — and the legislature — by numerous vocal and influential business and civic groups, meant the legislature would not hear the end of the matter until it appointed a commission to say something about it. Perhaps there were those in the legislature who thought that this time the commission would submit its report, which would be duly noted and then hidden away, and the clamor would subside. But that was not what happened. This time, as occurred eighty-six years later at the time of the creation of the Adirondack Park Agency, whatever might have been the politicians' wish for the report, it spun off landmark legislation.

Sargent spoke out on the Adirondacks before his appointment by the legislature, so his sentiments were not unknown. Late in 1883 he addressed a state Chamber of Commerce committee which had been named to look into the condition of the Adirondack forests, saying that preservation appeared to be the only solution, given the lumber industry's demonstrated inability to police itself. This was an important statement, coming as it did from an individual who was committed to the idea of scientific forestry. And it was but one of many tributaries that fed the ever-growing freshet of sentiment for preservation through acquisition. This freshet inspired the legislature, early in 1884, to appoint a committee to "investigate and report a system of forest preservation." Sargent was asked to chair the committee.

Through the summer of 1884, Sargent and his fellow committeemen gathered information, and in the fall they issued their report. It was, writes Frank Graham, Jr. in *The Adirondack Park*, "a scathing indictment of the timber thieves, the lumbermen, and the railroads," who were, according to the committee, reducing the Adirondacks "to an unproductive and dangerous desert." The committee supported the idea of state ownership of the forests, but considered it impractical. Instead, in Graham's words, "it proposed means for protecting the state lands from fire, thievery, and overcutting and recommended the establishment of a Forest Commission" to oversee use of the forests.

This proposal was not well received in the legislature, despite general agreement in that body that something had to be done. In stepped the powerful Board of Trade and Transporation, intent on keeping the momentum rolling. A meeting of board members and sympathetic legislators produced a bill, one which negotiated the millrace of legislative politics with hardly a scratch and was signed into law by Governor David B. Hill on May 15, 1885. The most significant section of that law read, "The lands now or hereafter constituting the Forest Preserve shall be forever kept as wild forest lands. They shall not be sold, nor shall they be leased or taken by any person or corporation, public or private." The Forest Preserve was a reality.

* * *

The year 1885 was, of course, the beginning of the history of the Adirondack Forest Preserve. By 1892 the Forest Preserve had become part of the larger Adirondack State Park, and by 1894 it had been given the additional armor of the state's constitution, meaning that henceforth it would take not the stroke of a bureaucrat's pen but the approval of a referendum by the voters of the State of New York, following approval of the proposed amendment by two successive legislatures, to alter in any way the Forest Preserve or the law that created it. These steps were taken, essentially, because it became clear in short order after the establishment of the Forest Preserve that it was not a forceful enough tool to do its job. Passage of the 1885 law had meant the creation of a Forest Commission to monitor compliance with the law; one of its three politically appointed members was a notorious timber thief who did little to change the public's opinion of him during his scandal-ridden tenure. As for the other two, there is no indication that they had even the slightest idea what they were supposed to do. The Adirondack State Park and, to a greater extent, the "Forever Wild" amendment to the state constitution probably would not have been necessary had those at whom the 1885 law had been aimed abided by it.

The significance of the constitutional amendment was great, greater indeed than its creators had intended. Certainly it was not what Marsh, Colvin, Hough and Sargent had wanted. What it meant, simply, was that forevermore the Forest Preserve had legal protection not only from illegal or imprudent timber harvesting but also from any lumbering or other resource development or human intervention in natural processes. The Forest Preserve was henceforth to be not a managed forest, but a wilderness untouched by man. The amendment prohibited "forest cultivation as practiced in Europe" and "using forest products as a source of revenue," as William Chapman White explained. These ideas had been the cornerstones of the grand plan developed by Marsh and his intellectual descendants. Surely they must have felt, even with the evidence before them, that the pendulum had swung too far. Perhaps they also saw that it had had a strong push.

From time to time, the voters of the state have approved amendments to the Forest Preserve article of the constitution. One such amendment permitted the construction of the Whiteface Memorial Highway. But more often, the voters have turned back attempts to compromise the Forest Preserve. No doubt they recognize that the Forest Preserve is a truly unique piece of the heritage of all New Yorkers.

Epiloque:
One Man's Forever Wild

GARY RANDORF

January 1

Wilderness — as long as I have lived in the Adirondacks, I have always been amazed at what lies right outside my back door. From my house in Keene I can ski or snowshoe unencumbered in practically any direction. What a gift it is to live in such a place and be involved with helping to protect it. I think more people have come to realize that it takes conscious effort and planning to ensure that wilderness will always exist here.

Out my back door it is an easy snowshoe to Corliss Point. As from many lesser-known hills, the view is remarkable. Why do so many people climb just the High Peaks, the mountains 4,000 feet and over?

The Adirondacks provide a wilderness backdrop. The mountain summits are heavily blanketed with snow, the air is frigid. A little snowshoeing warms you up quickly, however. No matter what kind of day it is, I am always glad I ventured out. The beauty of the Adirondacks cannot be masked by any weather.

Redpolls scrounge cheerily for weed seeds in the garden. Getting into the woods has made me as happy as the birds seem to be. I vow to get outside at every opportunity this year.

January 5

Thoreau said, "The question is not what you look at but what you see." Being in the Adirondacks helps us to see things clearly because the turning of the world, the will of nature, is so visible. Nothing gives me greater satisfaction than improving upon my own ability to see and then helping others to see as well. To see is to understand, to know, to cherish. Helping people to see is the first step in winning more support for the wilderness.

I'm teaching a course in winter nature photography; I take the class to the East Branch of the Ausable River near Keene. There is little snow, so we search the river's edge for frost and ice patterns. I've been harping on how important it is to get beyond just looking if you are truly to see things. Seeing, contrary to looking, should peel back the layers of things so that we can get to that which is within. I seem to do this best behind the lens of my camera, constantly looking for images that portray the ordinary as something new and fresh or beyond realism. The eye of my camera brings me closer to nature and always makes it more exciting. Now and then a scene, design, color combination, or lighting condition appears like an important discovery. Eureka!

February 10

Snow — since becoming an adult, but before I moved to the Adirondacks, I always thought of snow as something of a pain. Brought up in the snow belt of western New York, I dreamed of moving to warmer climes, and I did after college. But I am glad I have returned to the North Country, because I feel more alive experiencing the seasons, and the mountains and forests are never more beautiful, I now realize, than when they are blanketed with snow.

What a luxury it is to live in the Adirondacks and pick perfect winter days to play in the snow. A friend and I decide to do a "ski-shoe" trip to the summit of Phelps Mountain in the High Peaks Wilderness. This means using cross-country skis until the trail gets too steep, and then swapping them for snowshoes that we have strapped on our backs.

Skiing up the truck trail to Marcy Dam is sheer pleasure as the trail has been broken and the going is easy. Friendly chickadees at Marcy Dam come to us seeking food, and eat nuts and seeds right out of our hands. At the base of Phelps we make the switch to snowshoes and stash the skis in a snowbank. The trail to the top is short but steep, and we are pleased that our snowshoes are without tails and have crampons attached to keep us from slipping backward. The view of distant mountains is highlighted by Mount Marcy, whose summit is courted by clouds. Once we return to our skis, it seems like cheating to glide so effortlessly.

February 18

Snow makes me feel like a kid again — back when we rolled in it, ate it, and threw it at each other. During my first winter in the Adirondacks, a group of us skied to Owen and Copperas Ponds in the Sentinel Wilderness on a perfect, sunny day. We doubled over with a joyous freedom. I felt as if we all had gone back in time and forgotten we were adults.

I join the High Peaks Audubon group on a ski tour in the Santanoni Tract near the southwestern corner of the High Peaks Wilderness. The five-mile ski over a woods road to Newcomb Lake is one of the notable Adirondack trips. The conditions are perfect, and we are "high" on snow. Our lunch is GORP — good ole' raisins and peanuts (plus whatever) — and hot mulled wine, which we consume huddled on the porch of the "great camp," Santanoni. The return trip takes us across the lake, then on an esoteric bushwhack through woods and swamp. The Chapman family, who live in nearby Newcomb and know the country, guide us. We see little in the way of wildlife, but it has been a good day to study tracks in the snow and to gain a little more knowledge of the invisible wildlife's winter travel.

March 3

Someone has said, "Wilderness without wildlife is simply scenery." In the Adirondacks, seeing the large mammals is not easy. This is not really prime deer country, and black bears are quite shy. An encounter with a coyote happens infrequently, and a sighting of a bobcat is a rarity. Yet, seeing small mammals and birds can greatly enrich the wilderness experience. I have gotten people hooked on bird watching by simply handing them my binoculars at the right time.

Four of us, including expert biologist Greenleaf (Greenie) Chase, set off in pursuit of a northern (ladderback) three-toed woodpecker that has been sighted near Lake Clear. This is one of two Adirondack boreal birds that I've been dying to see. (The other is the spruce grouse.) Although we see fresh flecking of bark at the base of some dead trees, our confidence pales after we have stomped through brush and swamp for a couple of hours. And then at one of our stops, a member of our party hears, even if only barely, what can only be a tree's bark being flaked off. It is several minutes before we spot a female (lacking the golden crown) methodically stripping a dead spruce to find woodboring beetles. Alaskan Indian legend has it that the male devoured his mate in time of famine and wiped his paws clean on the top of his head. Proof? That yellow mark, that golden crown, which the male, but not the female, sports even today.

March 16

To want to climb the highest is human nature, so Mount Marcy will always be a big attraction. Yet I have done my best to steer away from Marcy, particularly during the peak hiking season, and head for mountains, which, besides being just as rewarding, offer better opportunities for solitude. I once suggested to a youth camp group that they try a lesser known mountain, and they have been going back there every year since, enjoying a place where they can encounter fewer people.

The dawn breaks crystal clear. It is a perfect day to go up Marcy, the highest peak of the Adirondacks and over a mile above sea level. A trip this time of year means fewer people and not having to deal with muddy trails. I reach the trailhead at 8 a.m., a good time because this is a fourteen-mile round trip on skis and snowshoes. Only one other person has signed the register ahead of me this day. He is an acquaintance who signs as the "Lone Ranger." Neither he nor I will erode the trail today. We will leave only a couple of tracks in the snow.

Several times on the way up I tramp side-by-side with yet other skiers. They have skins on their skis to help them up the steep grades and to slow them down on the descent. One of them is about on par with me as a skier, and he hollers like a banshee on the way down as he crashes off into the woods. Next time, says he, he'll hang up the skis and take snowshoes. The birds are quite active, and I see downy woodpeckers, pine siskens, purple finches, and a solitary brown capped, or boreal, chickadee.

April 10

I am sure that in most of us there is the urge to be an explorer. I am never happier than when I explore new country and mountains for the first time. Such was the case on this day.

Easter Sunday. Bright and sunny. A fitting day to celebrate on a mountain. Catamount Mountain, set down in a chunk of New York State Forest Preserve land in Clinton County, is the choice. I've sent people there who want a fine view from an open summit that is off the beaten path and doesn't require too much effort. We bushwhack straight north from the Forestdale Road, around to the north side of the summit, and then to the top and across to the highest point. Grand views are had of the Stephenson Range and Whiteface to the south, Taylor Pond and Silver Lake and rolling hills to the north, and the Jay Range and Lake Champlain to the east. Although there are four or five feet of snow on the north side, there is almost none on the south-facing slope; the spring sun is taking its toll. Behind a ledge and out of the wind we enjoy our lunch, and then we bushwhack down the steep southwest corner. Nearby is Silver Lake Mountain, another place I hope to explore soon.

May 5 and 6

Exploring an area's rivers and streams is one of the finest ways to get to know it. When I was asked to help study and evaluate the rivers of the Adirondack Park for possible inclusion in the state's system of wild, scenic, and recreational rivers, I couldn't have been more excited. I was not disappointed. It was one of the greatest experiences of my life. My partner most of the time was Clarence Petty, Adirondack native and the man who probably knows the Forest Preserve better than anyone alive. No matter how far we got into the back country, Clarence had been there before.

I join another staff member of the Adirondack Park Agency in a canoe trip along the Osgood River near Paul Smiths. The Agency must report to the state legislature whether this river should or should not be added to the Wild, Scenic, and Recreational Rivers System.

The upper section of the river, from the outlet of Jones Pond to two and a half miles downstream of Osgood Pond, is a fine flatwater paddle along expansive wetlands. We see an osprey, a beaver, three beaver lodges, sharp-skinned and red-tailed hawks, hooded mergansers, black ducks, mallards, a great blue heron, kingfisher, gray jay, and spotted sandpiper. These we record along with information on vegetation, land ownership, stream and streambed characteristics, and other pertinent data. We meet an elderly couple scooting proudly along in their new thirteen-foot aluminum canoe. It's fun to see people of all ages enjoying this country.

A second day takes us along the other canoeable stretch of the Osgood River, from the truck trail near Mountain Pond to Meacham Lake. That uncommon wildflower, the beautiful and redolent trailing arbutus, carpets the river banks in places, and the surrounding country is notably scenic and wild. I know now why Paul Jamieson, in his *Adirondack Canoe Waters: North Flow*, calls this "one of the most delightful cruising streams in the Adirondacks." He goes on to say that "its shores are varied in vegetation and contour, rising steeply in piny eskers and flattening in spruce and tamarack swamps, sphagnum bogs, or swales of grass, alders, and backwater.... It is rich in interest to the amateur botanist, geologist, and ornithologist or to any lover of uneven ground and moving water."

June 5

Adirondack roads can take you to as fine a country as you will see anywhere. I always take a camera along on my travels, and I jump out of the car whenever I see something of interest. Some of my most successful photographs have been taken from the roadside. I hope the gravel roads that wind through the woods will never be improved; they lead the way to experiences that are becoming harder and harder to find.

You don't have to climb a mountain or paddle a river to enjoy the Adirondacks. A drive home from Speculator proves it. At the Jessup River crossing on Route 30 I see my first parula warbler. At the Lake Durant Swamp near Blue Mountain Lake, a short walk from the car produces sightings of magnolia and yellowthroat warblers, kingfisher, and kingbird. South of Tupper Lake a drive along the Sabattis Road leads to a common loon on Little Tupper Lake. A bit farther north an old gravel pit bordered by a black spruce/tamarack bog yields cotton grass, Labrador tea, and pale laurel, all in bloom. A walk around its perimeter fails to turn up a spruce grouse, but a Canada warbler greets me eye-to-eye seven or eight feet away. The roadsides are carpeted by starflower, Canada mayflower, Clintonia, bunchberry, dogwood, and interrupted and sensitive ferns.

July 7

The Giant-Rocky Peak Ridge trip is hard to beat. Though I've done it only a couple of times, I think about it as much as any stretch I have taken, and I have travelled over these high country paths numerous times in my imagination. This may be as close to heaven as I'll ever get. But it was *hot* that day — so hot I don't think any of us was the least bit shy when we shed clothes to enjoy the coolness of that little mountain tarn, Lake Marie Louise.

Friends from Ithaca join us on a trip up Giant Mountain and Rocky Peak Ridge in the Giant Mountain Wilderness. A car dropped off at New Russia allows us to do a twelve-mile one-way trip through some of the most spectacular Adirondack country. It is a hard trip for a very hot day, but many are the rewards of outstanding mountain vistas to be had. As we ascend, I gauge our elevation by the thrushes I hear. First there is the woodthrush, then the veery in the hardwood forests. Higher up the hermit thrush calls, and when we progress even farther, a Swainson's thrush utters its flute-like song. Finally the uncommon gray-cheeked thrush chimes in where the upper spruce slope meets the sub-alpine zone. Twin flower, Clintonia, and bunchberry dogwood are just beginning to bloom in the high country, well beyond their prime flowering time at lower elevations.

We gently roll ourselves down off a ledge into eight-inch-deep Lake Marie Louise to get cooled off. It's rare not to find a refreshing breeze on the mountain summits. Rocky Peak Ridge was heavily burned over in the early 1900s, and little in the way of forest has returned. Trekking along this bare spine reminds me of hiking the Scottish Highlands.

August 6

Every time I go to the Pharaoh Lake Wilderness, one of my

favorite places, I think of the opposition that arose when the road to the lake was closed off so the area could be classified as wilderness. I know that some people were inconvenienced by the closing of the road, but there are just too few places in the world that offer what Pharaoh can when engines are shut off and left behind. More than once, one of my friends has carried a canoe three long miles into Pharaoh so that he could spend a week camped on one of its islands with one of his children. They gained experiences that will be with them for a lifetime, even if he did nearly break his back.

I head off into the Pharaoh Lake Wilderness, an imposing landscape of mountains and ponds between Schroon Lake and Ticonderoga. Crane Pond is brilliant in the sunshine, but I don't linger long because the top of Pharoah is my goal. It is the fire observer's last day, and the tower is to be put on reserve status. Most fire towers have been phased out of regular use as surveillance from aircraft has been found to be both effective and more economical. This is one of eight towers in wilderness areas that the 1972 State Land Master Plan deemed non-conforming. It is scheduled for phasing out and removal.

Although this finding caused some controversy, to the wild country enthusiast a tower, and even more particularly the telephone line that runs to it for miles through the woods, is surely out of place in a wilderness.

My return route is via Oxshoe, Crab, and Horseshoe Ponds. Oxshoe, bordered by large rocks and red and white pine on the northeast side, is particularly attractive, and one of its remote corners is fine for skinny-dipping. This is my first time in this year! The water is cool, about sixty-five degrees. The Pharoah Lake Wilderness offers some fine examples of northern hardwood forests of beech, yellow birch, and sugar maple, and although these are not virgin forests, one day they may again equal the grandeur of primeval forests because they are a part of New York's Forest Preserve.

August 13

Quiet is becoming harder to find as our world becomes more and more developed every year. It used to be that winter promised silence because it precluded motorized access to many places. But then came the snowmobile, and in some ways winter became the noisy season. With the advent of recreational vehicles that can go almost anywhere under any kind of conditions, it becomes even more important to have some country that is off limits to man's machines. When snow machines and motor boats were closed out of the St. Regis Canoe Area in 1972, the people of New York were given a rare and special gift.

My old boss from Westinghouse arrives from New Jersey to hike and canoe. Our first destination is the St. Regis Canoe Area, an 18,000 acre tract near Paul Smiths that contains numerous wilderness canoeing ponds. We set up camp on Little Long Pond in the shade of giant pines. After a swim, dinner, and tales by the campfire, we set off on the pond in moonlight. My urbanite friend has never

On Crane Mountain
Credit: Gary Randorf

"heard" such stillness, and he says it almost hurts his ears. How hard it is to find it in these times. I relish the thought of Adirondack trails that lead to quiet. There are some who cry out for making the wilderness accessible to motorized vehicles. No. Motors have their places elsewhere.

September 25 and 26

To help save the Adirondacks, it is essential to stay in touch with its back country. I have never felt guilty heading off into the woods on company time. When a trip is planned with the chairman of the Adirondack Council, I know it will not be cancelled, no matter what the weather. So, when the weather turned out well for this trip, it was like frosting on the cake.

The howls of coyotes wake me at 4:45 a.m. I always enjoy hearing them, and I fall back to sleep easily. Shortly after getting up at 8 a.m., I see the first flock of Canada geese heading for warmer climes.

I'm off on an annual mountain trek with two of the Adirondack Council's board members. From Elk Lake we head into Panther Gorge on the southern edge of the High Peaks Wilderness. Our goal is Mount Skylight. The trip is mostly uphill, and the eight-to-nine-mile trail seems long with a full pack. Not to miss an opportunity, though, I head for the summit of Haystack as soon as my tent is pitched and my sleeping bag and pad are rolled out. The view from the top of Haystack is awesome; many people rate this the top Adirondack peak for views. Twenty-seven major peaks and several water bodies can be picked out on a clear day. The sunset is perfection. Between photographs I munch on a peanut butter and jelly sandwich, pepperoni, and granola bars washed down with Tang. I scurry down, serenaded by two grey-cheeked thrushes along the way, and reach the tent before dark.

The following morning turns up a "bear story" from a couple camped across Marcy Brook. The night before, they were bedded down in their tent about a hundred feet from Uphill Lean-to between Lake Tear and Lake Colden. Two fellows in the lean-to were awakened by a bear sticking his head inside and snatching some food. Mr. Bear heads for the couple's tent, but, alas for him, their food is suspended from a limb by a cord. Undeterred, the bear climbs the tree, pulls the cache down and devours tuna fish, honey, and other goodies. And then he wanders off. The couple moves into the lean-to, figuring there is safety in numbers. They don't sleep much, however. One of the fellows is having nightmares, and till dawn he talks gibberish about giant bears. The moral of the story: don't panic; black bears rarely, if ever, harm campers. Tie your food up high and well, and hope.

October 18

Autumn may be the finest season in the Adirondacks, but every year I experience a sense of frustration when big game hunters are turned loose during a large part of the fall over all of the Forest Preserve. Some areas of the preserve should be closed to hunting so that the non-consumptive user can enjoy part of the autumn woods without worrying about the possibility of being shot.

Fog envelopes the woods, making subtle magic with the fading yellows and browns of autumn. The oaks are deep bronze, and the aspens are at their prime. We go for a drive along the Ausable River. The water is high, good conditions for a canoe trip for hardy souls. An osprey lights on a tree along the bank opposite the road. Near Wilmington we see a flock of migrating bluebirds. People are putting up storm windows and harvesting their gardens. I brought our onions and potatoes in last night and put them in the basement for storing.

After our ride, we start a fire in the Franklin stove. It is the start of the cozy season, for coming inside early to read and listen to music. The summer people have left. Many birds are following them south. Soon the hibernators will dig in, and soon the white stuff will come.

November 14

When late autumn rolls around, I think most others in the Adirondacks are ready and anxious for snow. What is more beautiful than the first wet snowfall that garlands all the trees and puts a hush all over the world?

The first real snowfall — about eight inches. I hope it sticks. I'm anxious to put "boards" under my feet once again and move off into the wilderness. Someone has just sent me some appropriate words from Sigurd Olson:

It may come on some quiet day in early November with a hush so profound it seems to press on everything. All living creatures feel it. They watch the skies and wait. Suddenly the air is white with drifting flakes, and tension drains as the ground is speckled with white. The first crystals rustle as they settle onto leaves and into crevices, and then almost magically the earth is white and winter has come.

December 29

"Peace on earth, good will toward men" is not something I just think about at Christmastime; it is a thought that often comes to mind when I have ventured out on winter nights. The snow and the winter light somehow make the world more awesome and a man feel smaller. It reminds me that we should be good to each other and to this earth we call home.

Two flying squirrels, whom we have named Orville and Amelia, are in our cedar slab bird feeder. They sure do a job wolfing down sunflower seeds. The little critters are about six inches long, and their tails are almost as long as that. They are reddish gray above and whitish beneath. Their noses are round, and they have large, expressive black eyes and rounded, almost naked, ears. In his *Natural and Civil History of Vermont*, originally published in 1842, Zadock Thompson described the habits of these elusive, aerial quadrupeds this way:

They usually inhabit the hollows of trees, and they feed upon nuts, grains, seeds, and buds. Their wings are not calculated for rising in the air

119

and flying in the manner of bats and birds. Consisting only of an extension of the skin of the flanks, they form only a kind of parachute, by which they are thus enabled to sail from one tree to another at a distance of several rods . . . . Their habits are nocturnal, and unless disturbed, they seldom leave their nests in the daytime.

Finally tired of watching the antics of the flying squirrels, I set off out our back door about midnight on a short ski. The lightly falling snow kisses my nose with a soft tickle. Now and again the moon hazily peeks through the hardwood trees on the slope west of the barn. All is at peace with the world.

On Cascade Mountain
Credit: Gary Randorf

About the Contributors

Neal S. Burdick is editor of publications at St. Lawrence University in Canton, New York, and a freelance editor and writer. A native of Plattsburgh, he has hiked, camped and cross-country skied in the Adirondacks all of his life. For three summers he was an instructor and administrator with the North American Wilderness Survival School at its Adirondack Base Camp, and for two summers he was a hutboy at the Adirondack Mountain Club's Johns Brook Lodge near Keene Valley. He is the editor of the Adirondack Mountain Club's Forest Preserve Series of Guides to Adirondack Trails, acting editor of the club's periodical, *Adirondac*, and book review editor of and a regular contributor to *Adirondack Life* magazine. He is also a member of the faculty of Potsdam State University College's Wilderness Workshop. He and his family live in a partially restored nineteenth-century farmhouse from whose study windows he can see the foothills of the northern Adirondacks.

Norman J. Van Valkenburgh has been employed for thirty years by the New York State Department of Environmental Conservation and its predecessor agency, the Conservation Department. He has served as chief of the Bureau of Land Acquisition, regional director of the department's seven-county Region 3 (lower Hudson Valley), and, for the last seven years, director of the Division of Lands and Forests. He is a licensed land surveyor in the states of New York and South Carolina. He is the author of *The Adirondack Forest Preserve: A Chronology*, published by the Adirondack Museum in 1979; *The Forest Preserve of New York State in the Adirondack and Catskill Mountains: A Short History*, published by the Adirondack Research Center at Union College in 1983; and *Land Acquisition for New York State: A Historical Perspective*, which will be published in 1985 by the Catskill Center for Conservation and Development. He has also written numerous articles on the subject of Adirondack and Catskill history.

William K. Verner, a resident of Long Lake, New York, in the heart of the Adirondacks, has been curator of the Adirondack Museum, editor of *Adirondack Life* magazine, consultant on the humanities to the National Fine Arts Committee of the XIII (1980) Olympic Winter Games, and chairman of the Citizens' Advisory Task Force on Open Space for the Adirondack Park Agency (1978-1980). He has written and lectured on American art, wilderness issues, and the Adirondacks, and has contributed articles on the Adirondack Park, the Catskill Park, and the New York State Forest Preserve to the *Encyclopedia of American Forest and Conservation History* (New York: MacMillan, 1983).

Philip G. Terrie teaches English and American Studies at Bowling Green State University in Ohio. He received an A.B. in English from Princeton and a Ph.D. in American Civilization from George Washington University. A former assistant curator at the Adirondack Museum, he has published several articles on Adirondack history. His book, *Forever Wild: Environmental Aesthetics and the Adirondack Forest Preserve*, was recently published by Temple University Press. He is currently book review editor of *Environmental Review*. He and his family spend their summers at their camp on Long Lake.

Warder H. Cadbury is a professor of philosophy at the State University of New York at Albany. Having spent his summers as a member of the family at Back Log Camp on Indian Lake, he has come by his interest in Adirondack literature and history quite naturally. The book by T. Morris Longstreth, *The Adirondacks*, published in 1917, was dedicated to his grandfather, Thomas K. Brown, the founder of Back Log. For nearly twenty-five years, Cadbury was a research associate for the Adirondack Museum. He has written introductions to reprints of W. H. H. Murray's classic *Adventures in the Wilderness* and John Todd's *Long Lake*. He is also the author of a biography of the artist Arthur F. Tait, who spent some thirty seasons in the Adirondacks, published this year by the University of Delaware Press and the *American Art Journal*.

J. Robert Williams was born at Trenton Falls and grew up in Prospect, where, he recalls, teamsters used to tether their great horses under the Union Hotel shed when they stopped for refreshment on their way to lumber camps in the West Canada headwaters country. Bob, who lives in Canton now, has been in and out of the Adirondacks for more than six decades. He tent-camped at Keene Valley in the 1920s, was boat boy at North Point Inn on Raquette Lake in the 1930s, laid siege to some unrewarding trout streams in the 1940s and '50s, climbed Mount Marcy for the first time in the 1960s, and since then has spent countless hours in his canoe in Adirondack waters, loafing and admiring the incomparable surroundings. He has been a reporter for the *Watertown Daily Times* and a public relations or public information officer for St. Lawrence University, Cornell University, and Oberlin College. Sometimes, in retirement, he does freelance writing.

Floy S. Hyde has spent a large portion of her life in the Adirondack Mountains. For thirty-five years she and her husband owned and operated a busy summer hotel, and it was out of this experience that she wrote her first history book, *Water Over the Dam at Mountain View in the Adirondacks*, published in 1970 and now in its third printing. This was followed in 1974 with *Adirondack Forests, Fields, and Mines*. Last year she published *Captain John Whipple*, the story and genealogy of a Rhode Island ancestor in the early 1600s. In addition to summer responsibilities in the Adirondacks, she served four years on the executive staff of the national Board of Education of The Presbyterian Church, U.S. and five years with the National Council of Churches of Christ in the USA. More recently she was for eight years associate professor of religion at Hartwick College in Oneonta,

New York. The recipient of many academic honors, Dr. Hyde was listed in the first edition of *Who's Who in American Women*.

Gary Randorf is executive director of The Adirondack Council. Previously, he was a natural resource planner and park naturalist with the Adirondack Park Agency. After spending time in a variety of professions, from plumber's helper to field superintendent in the Hawaiian sugar industry, he earned a master's degree in environmental education and natural resources conservation from Cornell University. Concurrently, he became involved in landscape and nature photography and environmental writing. He has been a contributor to *Adirondack Life, Living Wilderness, The Conservationist,* and other periodicals, and was the principal photographer represented in *Adirondack Wildguide,* published in 1984. He is currently working on two books: a photographic essay on the Adirondacks and a photographic journal dealing with America's coastlines. He is a member of the board of the Environmental Planning Lobby and a trustee of the Essex County Historical Society.